How To Make Good Decisions and Be Right All the Time

Also available from Continuum:

Great Thinkers A–Z, edited by Julian Baggini and Jeremy Stangroom

What Philosophers Think, edited by Julian Baggini and Jeremy Stangroom

What More Philosophers Think, edited by Julian Baggini and Jeremy Stangroom

The Good, the True and the Beautiful, Michael Boylan

What We Can Never Know, David Gamez

The Twenty Greatest Philosophy Books, James Garvey

A Brief History of Philosophy, Derek Johnston

What Don't You Know?, Michael C. LaBossiere

How to Win Every Argument, Madsen Pirie

How To Make **Good** Decisions and Be Right **All** the Time

Solving the Riddle of Right and Wrong

Iain King

continuum

Continuum International Publishing Group

The Tower Building
11 York Road
London SE1 7NX

80 Maiden Lane
Suite 704
New York, NY 10038

www.continuumbooks.com

British Library Cataloguing-in-Publication Data
A catalogue record for this book is available from the British Library.

ISBN-10: HB: 1-8470-6347-0
ISBN-13: HB: 978-1-8470-6347-2

Library of Congress Cataloguing-in-Publication Data

King, Iain.
How to make good decisions and be right all the time: solving the
riddle of right and wrong/Iain King.
p. cm.
Includes index.
ISBN 978-1-84706-347-2
1. Decision making–Moral and ethical aspects. I. Title.

BJ1419.K56 2008
170'.44–dc22

2008008279

Typeset by Newgen Imaging Systems Pvt. Ltd., Chennai, India
Printed and bound in Great Britain Cromwell Press, Trowbridge, Wiltshire
Cover photograph by Victoria King

Contents

Acknowledgements

Thoughts are odd things. They live through our words, in our minds and in our memories, but we never see them. We can see their effects, their shadows and sometimes the media which carry them, but never the thoughts themselves. Even when you 'grasp' a thought, you do not really hold it: grasping a thought means you understand its inner workings, usually through another thought, equally enigmatic.

So, although this book sets out a series of thoughts, it would be misleading to say I have full control over them. I take full responsibility for them, of course, including all the bad ones – the mistakes are all mine and mine alone, and I'm sure there are some (with every new error I find and correct, I fear there's another I'm yet to detect!). But the ideas in this book were moulded in my mind which was, in turn, affected by so many other people and experiences that it seems unfair to claim sole credit for any breakthroughs.

The experience which inspired this book more than any other occurred in September 1985, the year of Live Aid, when mass starvation in Ethiopia reached us through television. I visited Oxford for the first time and was appalled by the indulgent architecture of the inner court of the university's Bodleian library. Massive wealth had been devoted to the site, funded by the long-dead Earl of Pembroke whose pompous statue looked down on visitors. With full adolescent fury, I felt sure the money could have been spent so much better – why couldn't Oxford's wasted wealth be transformed into life-saving aid?

Although it seemed obvious that privileges should be given away as contributions, there was no formula to determine exactly how much everybody should give – finding the formula was an unsolved puzzle. I confided to friends that I would write a book on how resources should be shared out much more fairly, and so began my quest to find out what people, including myself, should do: half impassioned pursuit of justice, half intellectual treasure hunt.

There have been many meanderings since then, both intellectual and personal (this book answers my inner 14-year-old only in passing, in Chapter 37). But guided by the writings of Hume, Hare, Blackburn, Bentham, Mill and Kant, all of whom I owe a great intellectual debt, they have been fascinating meanderings. And learning from everybody who's taught me along the way, in my studies and in life, they have been as deeply formative.

Some writers describe their lives as solitary scrabblings for inner thoughts; others as perfect loneliness. My experience was neither, mainly because of the massive sociable support offered to me by so many generous friends. Thank you to the many people who have helped me with the many iterations of this book by commenting on drafts, inspiring me with ideas, providing me with a roof to write under or just being there when I needed it. I have just listed your names; I hope to thank you all for your contributions in person.

Arif Ahmed, Antonio Antiochia, Emma Back, Robert Baldock, Andy Bearpark, Simon Blackburn, Duncan Brack, Donatella Bradic, Helen Bridle, Jason Burke, Sarah Campbell, Duncan Clark, David Cloke, Alix Cohen, Tim Cooper, Tom Crick, Steve Cutler, Juliet Dowsett, Michael Dwyer, Daniel Elstein, Wyn Evans, Sarah Fradgley, Mary Gorwyn, Candida Goulden, AC Grayling, Monique de Groot, Martin Harris, Sue and John Hatt, Bjorn Hauksson, Roger M Haydon, Jane Heal, Oli Hein, Anna Helszajn, Richard Holme, Minna Jarvenpaa, Geoff King, Michael King, Victoria and Myles King, Rachel Lampard, Harvard Lillihammer, Andrew Lloyd, David Lunn, Linda Maclachlan, Myfanwy Marshall, Whit Mason, Ken Mayhew, Laura Mazal, Catherine McSweeney, Tania Mechlenborg,

Gay Meekes, Stella and Dick Messenger, Clare Mills, P. Muralidharan, John Naughton, the altruistic people of Novi Travnik, Lembit Öpik, Zbigniew Pelcynski, Robert Penman, Hilary Pennington and Wolfson College, Elizabeth Presse, Tatjana Radenkovic, Enisa Rashlanin, Ben Rich, Mark Russell, Chrissie Scanlon, Jo Shotton, Brendan Simms, Siobian Smith, Rebecca Sutton, Professor Marianne Talbot and the ever-inspiring weekly discussions in staircase 12, Mu Thomas, Lars Tummers, Besnik Vasolli, Victoria Whitford, Alex Wilcox, Andy Williams, Jenny and Alison Willott, Cynthia Wright, and my grandfather, William, whom I will never see again, but whose contribution included the most important advice of all: that anyone seeking to change the world should first think hard about how it can be improved.

Now this book is written, I don't know whether it quenches the pique of the 14-year-old who was once so revolted by that grandiose courtyard in Oxford; he's probably beyond help. Hopefully, though, this book can inspire anybody inflamed by the many tragic injustices of the world – to discover where the worst problems lie, to discuss how people can be helped to overcome them, and to do the right thing

Part I

The Problem: We Need to Make Decisions, But We Don't Know How

1 Five Challenges to the Formula of Right and Wrong

A few hundred years ago people were mystified by how things moved. They wondered what caused arrows and cannon-balls to make beautiful arcs as they flew across the sky. They watched planets move through the heavens. They speculated whether the 'music of the spheres' had a Divine cause; it certainly seemed beyond human explanation. There were a few clues: movement could be caused by people pushing or pulling things, and some things were easier to move than others. But there seemed to be no obvious link between the force applied and the movement that resulted. Some things needed a constant pull to maintain a constant speed, like a bucket of water drawn up from a well. Other things would speed up when you pulled them, like a stone in a sling. Others slowed down, like pulling on the reins of a horse. Moving things was an art, a matter of judgement and experience – there were no certain rules. When people wanted to move things, they had to rely on instinct or consult experts. They could never be precise.

But all that changed. Isaac Newton managed to explain movement with a few simple formulae. Mass, location, velocity and the force applied was all Newton needed to know. With these, he could calculate exactly how much any object would be affected by any sort of push or pull. He could predict how fast the object would go, and where it would be at any time in the future. Instinct and judgement were no longer necessary. The mystery was gone. Predicting movement had become Science.

Measuring right and wrong, like movement before Newton, is still a matter of art and judgement. People still rely on a mix of instincts and conventions, or they consult experts – traditionally religious authorities. Larger social questions of right and wrong are left to politicians, judges and grand committees chosen for their wisdom. It can take years of life experience to separate right from wrong, especially in the most difficult cases. Most of us have a vague sense of the important elements – there is something good about people who are honest, something bad about people who harm others, people who don't help others deserve less help themselves, and so on. But we are rarely precise. Some people even allow different rules for different people – it's OK for *them* to do that, but not for me.

Right and wrong need a Newtonian revolution. We need simple formulae so moral quandaries are no longer a matter of judgement or guesswork. We need an explanation of right and wrong so we don't have to rely on fallible experts to guide us. Once right and wrong is settled, debates about what should be done shrink into a discussion of what is happening in a situation because, with a formula, when you understand the situation you know what to do.

Unfortunately, the science of right and wrong is much more elusive than the science of movement. There are at least four reasons for this. First, movement is much easier to calculate. Movement depends on just four things: mass, location, velocity and the force applied. Right and wrong have many more than four things to fit into place (there are questions of motive, character, consequences, reciprocity and responsibility, to name just five). Second, there are already far too many opinions on right and wrong. To transform right and wrong into a science we need to prove most of these opinions are wrong, which is much harder than saying we disagree with them. Third, while we can test scientific formulae by observing results, how we test formulae for right and wrong is much less obvious. Finally, at the centre of right and wrong is ourselves, something we don't fully understand yet. We have to build a science around a kernel of mystery.

But, even though the problem is harder, the prize is much greater. Understanding movement may have inspired the industrial revolution, motor cars and space rockets, but understanding right and wrong is the key to much more. If we know what we should do, then we can make the world the best it can be. It means everyone can live a good life, do good things and be a good person. These goals may sound Utopian or a little ridiculous, but there is no reason to assume they are unattainable. People used to think there was something unattainable about perfectly precise movement. They don't think that now.

People have searched for this science before, of course. Indeed, the search for right and wrong is a story in itself – one that has occupied many scholars for hundreds of years and that is worthy of many books. Some attempts to define right and wrong have been beautifully simple, others more complicated. But the search was less rigorous than you might imagine: for many centuries the mystery of what to do was simply attributed to a mysterious God. Some of the earlier efforts to break free from organized religion got lost in questions of language and meaning, while others concluded there was no answer to be found. Now we have an answer we know what they were seeking. This book presents a unified explanation of right and wrong.

But an explanation is not enough. A good explanation needs a reason to back it up: it needs proof – proof that this is the only correct account of right and wrong rather than just another opinion. This means proof that all other accounts of right and wrong are in some way defective.

And the explanation needs something else, too. It needs to offer practical advice. People need to know what they should do in the real world, in the complicated dilemmas they face everyday when the ideal path is not open to them. A complex formula is of no use when people are trying to feed their children – their children will always come first, whatever the formula says. Any formula which ignores this is missing something.

Hence, sorting out right and wrong is not a single challenge – it is five, and it is around these five challenges that this book is set out.

First, we need to understand what's wrong with current theories about right and wrong. When you look at the way things are, all the crazy things people do and all the bad things that happen, something is clearly awry. But that is not enough: we need to know exactly where the fault lies. This first part of this book, up to Chapter 6, takes apart common notions of right and wrong, identifies the good bits and throws the rest away.

Second, the new formula for right and wrong needs a firm basis. We need a proof, an ultimate back-stop which can answer all the questions about why people should adopt this system of right and wrong over every other. The proof is vital because without it our explanation of right and wrong would be just another opinion. Chapters 7 to 14 provide this proof and identify the basic 'DNA' of right and wrong.

Third, the new formula must convert this firm basis of right and wrong into a clear guiding principle. When you read this book, you will see this central principle is the Help Principle. Here we can copy a trick from Newton, who stripped a problem down to its most basic elements, then considered the effect of changing each one in turn. We refine and define this Help Principle in the same way, by considering in turn the impact of variables like time, different intentions and chance. This is the third part, which runs to Chapter 22.

Fourth, the formula must be able to apply this central Help Principle to as wide a range of problems as possible. Chapters 23 and 24 deal with blame and punishment; Chapter 25 covers promises; Chapter 26 explains when we should lie; Chapter 27 deals with romance and sex; and Chapters 28 and 29 set out how to make the best decisions in groups. We need to know what to do in each of these scenarios, and that involves converting the Help Principle into clear advice for each situation. Answering this fourth challenge means a comprehensive programme explaining the best thing to do in many situations.

Finally, the formula must convert these core principles into practical advice for people living in the real world, so people know what to do when they can't do what's best. Chapters 32 to 38 explain that being good isn't for the pure-at-heart; it is something we all should do. This fifth part covers law, how much we should put family before strangers, when it's OK to do bad things, how to tackle poverty and how much each of us should give to charity. It also explains how different but equally valid accounts of right and wrong can emerge in different cultures, including when we should accept these differences and when we should confront them.

The overall approach of this book is straightforward: it is to examine the dominant theory of right and wrong, to identify its faults and virtues, and see how it can be altered so as to correct all the faults and keep all the virtues. But, although this approach is straightforward, it is not easy, because the new system has to be developed right from scratch – it requires a fundamental foundation, a proof. And, even if the faults in the old system can be corrected, the new theory has to be extended into many areas of human activity, each of which provides new tests and challenges.

This book is meant to explain rather than to offend. Nevertheless, if your views on right and wrong are based on religion in some way, then you might find this book disconcerting: this book explains right and wrong without it. Just as 'God' used to explain the mysteries about movement before they were explained by science, people have often used religion to explain the mystery involved in right and wrong. This explanation is not needed any more. Right and wrong can now be explained much more clearly without a Supreme Being. This doesn't mean it's bad to believe in God, and religion still covers plenty of spiritual and transcendental mysteries which remain untouched. But it does mean the various religious figures who try to instruct us, from preachers and imams to witch doctors and holy men, will have to rethink their arguments. Religions had to adapt their proclamations to survive Darwin's explanation of evolution; now they will have to alter their account of right and wrong if they are to be credible in the modern age.

If you are reading this book purely for advice, then there are many sections which you will find useful on their own. Go to Chapter 7 if you want to understand the meaning of life. Read Chapter 26 if you want to know when to lie. See Chapter 27 for rules on romance. Turn to Chapter 33 if you want to know which social conventions to challenge. Look at Chapters 36 and 37 to know how much to give to charity. Many months after you have finished this book, you will certainly want to refer back to it every now and again, especially when you have a difficult decision to make. The main conclusions are reprised at the end, in Chapter 40, for easy reference.

But too many books have dictated right and wrong before. If this book were merely another list of instructions, then there would be no more reason to follow it than any of its predecessors. It would be just another opinion. This book is more than that: it is a comprehensive system for discerning right from wrong, backed up with a proof and explanation. People need to read the whole book if they are to understand the reasons for doing something. You need to appreciate the ideas behind the ideas and the thoughts within the thoughts. Just as people can speak a language more thoroughly if they study the language's grammar, so too with right and wrong: people should understand what lies behind instructions, not just learn them by rote.

Most people feel a deep urge to do what is right, and almost everybody tries to justify their actions. Even when we admit we did something wrong, we try to find an excuse – we say too much was expected of us, we misread the situation or that some rules deserved to be broken. Only the most selfish of sociopaths has no concept of right and wrong. Everybody else, the vast majority of us who refer to right and wrong on most days, needs to understand the concepts we are using, or frequently misusing.

And there is a desperate need for us to do what is right. So much goes wrong because people behave badly. People are ignored, people are abused and people die, all unnecessarily. Think of all the bad things in the world and how much better they would be if people behaved better. Most people would behave better if they just knew how.

So, if you want to make the world a much, much better place, then you should read on. If you've ever wondered what you should do in a particular situation, then you should read on. And if you've ever wanted to make better decisions, then you should read on.

But especially, if you don't like taking advice at face value because you want to know *why* you should do certain things, then this book is for you.

2 Desperately Seeking a System

Here are three problems caused by the way people behave:

- Sven lives in a dictatorship, a cruel regime kept in power by the notoriously brutal interior police. He has been offered a senior position with the police. Sven hates the regime, but he knows that if he turns down the job the vacancy will be filled by Erik, who enjoys being nasty. Should Sven work for police service and help prop up the regime? Or should he allow Erik to take the job, knowing that Erik will work hard for the interior police and make the police even more brutal?
- Sue has agreed to go to a dance with John. John has bought her ticket and is looking forward to the event. Now, though, Sue has been invited by Steve, with whom she would much rather go. Should she take up Steve's offer and upset John? Or should she keep her promise to John, and miss out on an evening with Steve? Whatever she does, should she lie to either of them?
- Approximately six thousand children in the world die every day from diarrhoea – well over 2 million a year. Many of these deaths could be prevented if facts about basic hygiene were more widely understood and if more money was spent on providing clean water in developing countries. How much should a rich person in a distant, developed country give to stop these children dying of diarrhoea? Should they support other causes too? How much should *you* give?

These are not random problems: they summarize the search for answers at the beginning of the twenty-first century.

Sven's problem is based on a dilemma posed about 30 years ago by the English philosopher, Bernard Williams, called 'George the Chemical Scientist'. George, like Sven, could either take a job with a nasty organization or he could allow the job to go to someone else who would do the nasty work even more enthusiastically. Williams concluded there was no simple answer to this dilemma, so therefore certain simple explanations of right and wrong could be ruled out.

Sue's problem could have been taken from one of the many 'problem pages' published in magazines for teenagers every week. It evokes the more human side of right and wrong, and reminds us that seeking the right answer is not an abstract, academic exercise. Everybody needs advice – it's part of the fabric of life.

The final problem is as much political as it is personal. It's the focus of the massive 'Make Poverty History' campaign of 2005, and many similar campaigns which have come before it. There is not yet an answer to this problem, and terrible poverty is still with us; if the problem is solved then poverty may be banished.

What should Sven do about the job with the police? What should Sue do about the dance? What should everybody do about the six thousand children dying every day from diarrhoea?

There are clear answers to these questions, as we shall see. But before we reach them, we can see the questions themselves already provide some revealing facts. Sven is a good person, so is Sue, and we all care deeply about the children dying of diarrhoea. Yet, despite these good intentions, bad things are happening. Either Sven will take a job which supports a cruel regime, or Erik will make the regime even worse. Either Sue will break a promise to John, or she will miss out on an evening with Steve. Meanwhile, we have all failed to prevent thousands of children dying from an easily preventable disease. By any fair measure, these are all bad things. Most people are good, but we still allow bad things to happen. Why?

If you look at the world around you, and think of other examples of good people allowing bad things to happen, an answer soon becomes obvious: the central reason good people allow bad things to happen is that we don't know what to do. This applies to Sven, Sue and everybody else who tries to be good. We're not sure what being good actually involves. But that doesn't mean there is nothing we should do in these situations: we need a system for making decisions, *whatever situation we face*. We need to know what is right and what is wrong, even when the best course of action is not available to us.

This is important for three reasons. First, it makes 'right' and 'wrong' adaptable to bad situations, so we know what to do in the imperfect world in which we live. Whatever Sven or Sue do, there will be something awkward about their choice. It's not enough to say there is 'no right answer'; that doesn't help them very much. Sven and Sue need advice.

The second reason we need a system for making decisions is to settle our minds. Sven and Sue are in disturbing situations. Even if they do what is right, there is a danger they will regret it or feel guilty, because their situation will have forced them to do something which seems wrong in some way. A system for making decisions can dispel this sense of guilt or regret. It can give people confidence that they did the right thing. Guilt and regret are not irritants to be remedied as you might dispel a headache with a painkiller; they need to be dispelled in a proper way, by doing what is right.

The third reason we need a system for making decisions is so we can set priorities. Is it more important to go to war or save a plant threatened with extinction? Should we tackle poverty or disease? It's not just a case of doing what's right. We need to know which right thing is most important.

Without a comprehensive system for making decisions, most people have adapted their own way of responding to bad things. As the Roman Empire collapsed, some people called 'Stoics' took a fatalistic approach to the problems of the world, and concerned themselves just with their own actions, narrowly defined. In the Middle Ages, many people thought they could 'purify' themselves by obtaining holy artefacts, even if they had done evil things. In modern times, when told of the preventable deaths caused by diarrhoea, most people wince and express sorrow, but return within a few minutes to the everyday concerns which dominate their lives. 'Condemn but remain cosy' is the most widespread response to problems in the modern world.

These responses may seem weak, but before we condemn them in turn, we need to understand why they arise. When people are bombarded by daily news of tragedy which has no obvious answer, why shouldn't they just 'condemn but remain cosy'? What *is* the alternative? It's this alternative we must find, and urgently.

3 Unreliable Advice from Religion and Dice

Luke Rhinehart has a system for making decisions, although it is a distinctly odd one. It is a system which is simple, can be applied very widely and can enable people to escape the confines of their boring lives. Some say the system has become a cult; it certainly seems dangerous. Although it has inspired adventure and creativity, it has also inspired murder and rape. The system told Luke Rhinehart to seduce his neighbour, release psychiatric patients and leave his family. He is Dice Man, and he makes important decisions by rolling dice.

Rhinehart, of course, is fiction, but the book in which he set out his dice system, *Dice Man*, was one of the most fashionable books of the early 1970s, and perhaps one of the most influential of the century. The system for making decisions is simple: list your options, give them numbers, roll dice and choose whichever option the dice dictate. A theatre production based on the book still runs – in line with the theme of the performance, theatre-goers roll dice to determine the price of their tickets. The system of dice rolling has been taken up on television programmes, where adventurers use dice to decide where to travel next, and Rhinehart's approach can be adapted to many other situations. Perhaps it could be applied to everything.

But would *you* trust it? Would you decide which job to take, who to marry or where to live, just on the roll of a die? Most people want their system for making decisions to be based on more than just chance.

We don't trust Rhinehart's dice because we want our decisions to be *right*.

There are lots of systems for making decisions. Sven, Sue and anybody else who needs advice can easily find people who are prepared to offer it. The Dice Man's advice is nakedly random; many other systems are more subtly so. The challenge is to find *good* advice. We want advice which we can rely on to be good.

Most children look to authority figures when they seek advice. They ask their parents or a teacher when they don't know what to do. This approach has something going for it: parents and teachers often understand the world better than children, and they may understand a child's interests better than the child. Sven and Sue, though, are already adult. They have thought their problems through and are fully aware of the options they are choosing between. Asking another adult won't help them much.

Adults have traditionally sought expert advice from religious figures, and many people still do today. Religion deals with mysteries – where we came from, what happens to us when we die and the peculiar spiritual awareness many people feel. Many religions offer answers when there is mystery about what we should do, too.

Religion-based systems for making decisions exist in most cultures. Most involve seeking holy advice, either by contacting a God directly, or by interpreting texts or other signs associated with Him; people are then expected to obey this advice because of its Divine source. The more advanced religions have elaborate codes which tell people what to do, often written down in some detail.

The trouble is most religions offer advice which contradicts itself, and advice which tells you to do two opposite things at the same time can never be followed. Christianity, for example, may say Sven should be 'true to himself', which presumably means not joining the brutal interior police; at the same time, the same religion might tell him to 'take responsibility for his actions', which means he should take the job, to keep out Erik. Sue, meanwhile, is forced to choose between upholding her promises, and acting on a God-given emotion. Sven and Sue cannot do both these things, so they cannot follow the advice. Contradictory advice is no advice at all.

When a religion or a holy text offers contradictory advice – as it probably would for Sven and Sue – experts, such as priests and holy men, are asked for their interpretation. This means it is the experts, not the religion itself, who set the rules when a religion is unclear. If a religion needs lots of interpretation, then the experts can become very powerful. That is not necessarily bad – they may be very good experts. But it does mean that whether the experts are good cannot be determined by God or the holy text anymore. What constitutes 'good' must lie elsewhere.

Even if there were a religion which did not contradict itself or require expert interpretation, most religions contradict each other. Muslims often advocate arranged marriages, a system modern Christians reject. Jews say it's wrong to eat shellfish, Hindus say it's wrong to eat cows and some Buddhists say it's wrong to eat any animal. How do we choose which religion offers the best advice?

We cannot ask the religions themselves. All religions claim to be the True Religion. They all claim Divine Origins. Checking out their historical credentials also yields little to help us decide between them.

We might try to choose which religion to follow by seeking to contact God Himself. Many people who are touched by religion claim to be able to communicate with Him directly. For some, this is a vaguely spiritual feeling, for others it is a much stronger almost physical sensation and for a few it is a clear voice in their heads. But this still doesn't offer much to choose between religions: if more than one version of God can be contacted this way we are no further forward, and some of the instructions received in this way are disturbing – warmongers and psychopaths have often received 'advice from above'.

Some people argue religion has a place in determining right and wrong through a sort of consensus approach. They sense a profound awareness of the beauty of the world and a mysterious benevolence towards other people which makes them want to take their interests into account. This is perhaps the dominant defence of religion today: most religions say we should be nice to each other, and the mysterious feeling of benevolence seems so real, so why *not* follow religious advice? How could anybody argue we *shouldn't* obey God by being nice to one another?

This is a deceptive argument: many people *do* feel a mysterious benevolence; most religions *do* say we should be nice to each other; and being nice to each other *is* indeed at the heart of doing the right thing. But the first two facts do not lead to the third. The only way to form a consensus of religions is to leave some out: a consensus of religions which were all benevolent would have to exclude the Aztec faith, for example, because Aztecs worshipped the ripping out of human hearts. How do we decide which religions to ignore? Either we draw up a consensus by choosing only 'nice' religions – which gets us nowhere ('religions which say we should be nice to each other say we should be nice to each other'), or we must choose between religions by using some other measure.

Even if religions did converge towards a consensus, they could still be wrong. A consensus of people once thought the earth was flat. A consensus of people used to think there was nothing wrong with slavery. Great religious figures, like Jesus and Mohammed, were outside consensus opinion and proved their greatness by confronting it. Any consensus today that God says we should be nice to each other could be wrong in the same way.

Does the mysterious sense of benevolence compel us to follow religious teaching? No. People experience other mysterious sensations, which can be just as powerful – such as paranoia, infatuation and depression. We could find a religion to advocate for each of these – some ancient civilizations even had a God for each one; religion does not give us a reason why benevolence is most important.

There is a common conclusion emerging here: choosing which religious advice to follow must require something other than religion.

If there is a place for religion in determining right from wrong, we must step away from religion to find it. Even if religion is good, it cannot tell us what good is.

This does not mean religion is always bad. Religions represent centuries of accumulated wisdom, and we would be unwise to jettison it entirely. Many religious people are very noble. Religions are often at the forefront of charitable efforts. They can bolster communities, provide solace to people who need it and help people think through confusing issues of right and wrong. But most, perhaps all of these can be done even better without a religious element. If 'God is Love', as Jesus said, then we might be better off just concentrating on 'Love', and cutting out the middle Man. This problem was first identified by Plato, who asked 'Is an action right because God commands it?' If it is, then doing what is right means simply following the demands of a dictator; if not, and God commands something because it is right, then we can ignore God's commands, and just do what is right.

Religion has provided more than a distraction from right and wrong over the years. It has inspired murderous jihads and crusades, induced great hardship in a mistaken pursuit of spiritual enlightenment and allowed people to overlook terrible injustices. Some modern cults are little more than power pyramids which allow those at the top to abuse those further down. Clearly, some of the things religions do are good, and some are bad. The point is: we need something independent of religion to decide which is which.

The trouble is, if we can't base right and wrong on God, then what can we base them on? Nietzsche, accused by some of being the philosophical father of Nazism, thought right and wrong meant nothing without religion. 'If God is dead,' he wrote, 'then everything is permitted'.

Sven and Sue could get advice from plenty of other places: politicians, tarot-card readers, magazine columnist or, if they are prepared to take a risk, from Dice Man. But none of this advice will help them much. Whatever any of these people say, there is still no obvious reason to do what they say.

Most developed societies have laws which offer fairly clear advice on things. If there were a law covering Sven's situation, or Sue's, then they could follow it. Also, most laws are reasonably consistent: when two laws offer contradictory advice, there is usually a well-established legal remedy to resolve the problem. The trouble is that laws don't really offer advice for Sven and Sue. They deal with what you *must* do, which is different from what you *should* do – especially in an authoritarian society, like Sven's, where many laws are brutally wrong. Laws are drafted by people, so taking advice from them amounts to little more than taking advice from law-writing experts: better than nothing, but it does not tell us what laws those experts should draft.

So, of the many systems for making decisions, none seems to offer a truly convincing reason to adopt them, and some are little better than rolling dice. Is this all we can offer Sven, Sue and everybody else who has to make a difficult decision? Is there a better way to produce advice?

There is.

4   The Enlightenment Decision-Making Machine: Do Whatever Is Best . . .

Once Newton had worked out his formulae for calculating movement, several thinkers tried to apply his scientific methods elsewhere, hoping to use observation and logic to improve the world around them. This approach may seem obvious now, but back then it was heresy. Power and ideas, which had always been inherited from the previous generation without question, were challenged for the first time in centuries. The subversive voice of reason became a conversation. Words rose into a clamour for action. Traditions which couldn't be justified had to be changed. This was the Enlightenment, and it eventually led to revolutions in industry, music, mathematics, and political revolutions in America and France.

The Enlightenment produced a new system for making decisions, too. Drawing on a long heritage which can be traced back to ancient Greece, where Aristotle developed an austere version of the theory, the early Enlightenment philosophers John Locke and David Hume developed the idea, preparing the way for the radical writer Jeremy Bentham to define it with a book in 1789. Echoing one of Newton's greatest achievements, Bentham called his system a 'calculus' for determining right from wrong. Indeed, he had described a process which could be applied without any human judgement at all: it was a decision-making machine. Since then, the system has come to dominate all the others. It is a system now used very widely – by economists, politicians, civil servants, parents, doctors, emergency workers, conservationists, engineers and architects. It is a system used for designing roads, and deciding how fast cars should be allowed to drive. It is a system used by people who draft laws, and sometimes by the justice system which enforces them. It is a system used in warfare and in military hospitals. It can easily advise Sven and Sue, and those of us wondering how to help the thousands of children dying of diarrhoea. It even seems to be a scientific system for making decisions, somehow guaranteed to advise what's best. And it is a system with the virtue of being very simple.

The system for making decisions is this: *do whatever is best*. 'Do whatever is best' is really very straightforward. It means you look at all the things you could do, decide which will bring about the best consequences and do it.

So, when it comes to designing a road, there are two basic options: build it or don't build it. Building the road will satisfy a certain number of car users, and you can estimate how much by asking them – what value would they put on the road? Not building it will save money that could be used elsewhere. You weigh the two options, and decide which is best. If the value justifies the cost, then you build it. If not, then you don't. If you decide to build the road, then you can use the same method to decide what route it should follow, how big it should be, and so on. Whatever the situation, you simply do whatever has the best consequences.

The phrase 'best consequences' is doing a lot of work here. What are the 'best consequences'? How should we decide what is best?

'Best consequences' can be decided in several ways. Jeremy Bentham, writing at the time of the French Revolution, suggested we should pursue the 'Greatest Happiness of the Greatest Number', but this formulation can be difficult – what if you have to choose between greater happiness and a greatest number? Nowadays, people tend to equate 'best' with 'most wanted'. The 'best consequences' means the outcome which is desired more than any other. It's a question of satisfying people as much as possible. Notice that it's not just a crude calculation of the numbers in favour versus the number against; the amount people want each option is important, too. Intense desires count for more than weak ones. If ten people want to build a road *very much*, and there are twelve people with only very mild objections, then the road should be built. 'Do whatever has the best consequences' involves choosing the option which produces the most satisfaction.

There is a beguiling logic to this system, identified by the Victorian philosopher John Stuart Mill. Mill asked: How could anybody want anything *but* the best consequences?

To see what he meant, think of a recent decision you made: perhaps something trivial, like a decision to buy one brand of toothpaste rather than another. You chose the toothpaste you eventually bought because you thought it was the best thing to do – correct? That doesn't mean it was the best toothpaste – you might have bought the cheaper brand to save money. Perhaps you saw it advertised recently, and thought you'd give it a try, not knowing whether it was best. The point is, when you factored in all the important parts of your decision – cost, availability, taste, the toothpaste's ability to keep your breath fresh, and so on – you tried to do what was best. You tried to do whatever had the best consequences. If that's how we make decisions alone, then, according to Mill's beguiling logic, that is how we should make decisions together. With several people, it's simply a case of taking everybody's interests into account rather than just one person's. We're not just buying toothpaste for ourselves any more. Now we're shopping for the whole family (or, in the case of government, the whole country). We're trying to do what's best for everybody, not just ourselves. So, said Mill, we should do whatever's best, because we naturally try to do what's best anyway. We shall return to Mill's proof later.

There's something very appealing about the idea we should do whatever has the best consequences – it seems to capture something important. If you are on a ship, and you see someone struggling in the water, then 'do whatever has the best consequences' will advise you to help them. You might throw them a floatation ring. The ring may be cold and wet, and a completely selfish person wouldn't touch it. But 'do whatever has the best consequences' means you have to take account of the person struggling in the water, too. They need the ring much more than you need to keep your hands warm and dry. So you throw them the ring. Simple.

(This, we shall see later, is the basic Help Principle. The Help Principle says you should help someone if your help is worth more to them than it is to you. A basic form of the Help Principle is at the core of 'do whatever has the best consequences'.)

There are three unfounded objections commonly made against the system 'do whatever has the best consequences'. These objections are important, but they are not nearly as important as some people make out. They certainly do not kill off the idea of 'do whatever has the best consequences'.

The first objection is this: it's hard to compare how much different people value things. You can never know what it's like to be struggling in the water unless you are actually there. Similarly, if you are designing a road, you can never know how much other people really want or don't want the road. If you ask them, they are sure to exaggerate their wishes to get their way. Comparing what different people want and choosing between them is very difficult.

Yes it is difficult to make these sorts of comparisons between people, but that doesn't undermine the system. Comparing what different people want and choosing between them is a vital social skill, developed in people from their earliest experiences in the playground. It is hard to get right, and very hard to do perfectly, but that's not a fatal flaw.

Also, practitioners of 'do whatever has the best consequences' have evolved clever ways to cope with this problem. Doctors have used 'do whatever has the best consequences' in military hospitals since the age of Napoleon. When not all casualties can be treated, they are separated into three groups. The first group is made up of the walking wounded whose life doesn't depend on receiving treatment; the second group are the critical cases whose life *does* depend on it; and the third group are those who will die whatever happens. Doctors then concentrate on the middle group, to save as many lives as possible. This system of 'triage' involves comparing very varied injuries. But these comparisons are not too difficult: certain sorts of wounds put people in certain categories. There will always be borderline cases, but that doesn't invalidate the whole system.

Other professions use different systems. Accountants try to make these comparisons between people by measuring value for money. Architects try to compare the extra beauty of a design feature with the extra cost. Teachers try to make the best use of their time between the different students in their class. Making comparisons between people is not always easy, but lots of people do it. Hence, this objection is more of a practical problem than a real difficulty. It is something for people to tackle, not to make them change direction.

The second objection against the 'do whatever has the best consequences' system is about the way decisions are made. This accusation, made by Bernard Williams in the 1970s, is that it gives people 'one thought too many'. If you are on the ship, Williams said, and you see the person struggling in the water, you shouldn't do a calculation before you act – you should just save them! Calculating how much the person in the water wants the ring, then calculating how wet and cold the ring is, then comparing the two, then doing the sums and only finally deciding you should help the person in the water seems wrong. (For a start, you might take so long that the person drowns while you're thinking!) 'Do whatever has the best consequences' takes the spontaneity and impulse out of doing good.

This objection is based on a misinterpretation. 'Doing whatever has the best consequences' doesn't involve doing sums while a person drowns, and the best way to explain this is by comparing being good with speaking a language. You can learn a language better if you also learn the underlying system of grammar, but you shouldn't think about pluperfect subjunctives and conditional tenses when you speak – it's too distracting. You just need to express yourself. Understanding grammar helps you to speak better, but it shouldn't be at the front of your mind. The same is true of 'doing whatever has the best consequences': people acting on this motto should rush to save the drowning person just like everybody else. They should have a better understanding of why they are rushing, but it shouldn't slow them down.

The third objection, made most recently by the Nobel Prize winning Indian economist Amartya Sen, is that 'do whatever has the best consequences' is unfair. It caters for the people who can be satisfied and ignores those who can't. Imagine you had a pair of top-of-the-range running shoes, and you had to decide whether to give them to an athlete or a person in a wheelchair. The person in the wheelchair won't be able to use them but the athlete can, so the best consequences mean giving the running shoes to the athlete. This *does* seem unfair – after all, the athlete is already lucky, they don't deserve something more. The misfortune of the person in the wheelchair is being compounded – they have already lost their mobility, now they are missing out on running shoes, too.

But Sen's objection is misleading. 'Do whatever has the best consequences' is only unfair because life is unfair. If it's possible to trade the shoes for something worth more to the wheelchair user, then the shoes should be traded. If no such trade is possible, then why *not* give the shoes to the athlete? It's the same decision faced by the triage doctor who must choose between helping a critically wounded casualty and a fatally wounded one. The misfortune of the fatally wounded casualty will be compounded by the fact he will be treated second. It's unfair in a way, but it means the critically wounded casualty is saved, and saving one life is better than saving none.

So there is something attractive about the idea of 'doing whatever has the best consequences'. It is used widely with much success, and three of the objections commonly raised against it shouldn't worry us.

So: did the Enlightenment thinkers get it right? Is 'do whatever has the best consequences' the system for making decisions we need?

5   . . . Does Not Seem Best

Magnetic compasses were developed in China and reached the Middle East and Europe around the thirteenth century. They revolutionized sea travel: ships no longer needed cloudless skies to navigate by the sun and stars, which meant they could sail during the Mediterranean winter for the first time, providing a massive boost to trade. The new technology helped explorers discover new continents. Navies with compasses were seriously better than navies without. Seafarers no longer needed judgement or a sense of direction; compasses provided those now. Just one small, simple device had transformed the whole business of sea travel. Compasses seemed wonderful.

But when sailors tried to find a sea passage from the Atlantic through the Arctic waters around Canada and into the Pacific, compasses mysteriously failed them – because they had ventured over the magnetic north pole. Ships with compasses still ran into dangerous rocks because they couldn't determine longitude. And when ships started to be made of steel, compasses could misdirect vessels badly. After many years and many shipwrecks, sailors gradually realized magnetic compasses were not, on their own, a reliable tool for sea navigation.

Some of the Enlightenment thinkers who advocated 'do whatever has the best consequences' believed they had found the ideal system of moral navigation. Simple and scientific, like a magnetic compass, the new formula gave clear direction that could be followed wherever people went. They thought they had found the perfect moral compass. Were they right – is 'do whatever has the best consequences' the system we need for making decisions?

Given that this book has 40 chapters, you are probably unsurprised to learn that the answer is 'no': doing whatever has the best consequences is not the perfect system. In fact, there are huge problems with it. But you may be amazed to find out just how flawed it is.

We need to know what these flaws are. The defects in the wrong system provide the clues we need to find the right one. Indeed, if we can identify all the faults with 'do whatever's best' and correct them, then we should have the system we need for making decisions.

To see what's wrong with 'do whatever has the best consequences', think back to Sven's dilemma. Sven has to decide whether to take the senior position he has been offered with the interior police. If he does, he will be propping up a cruel regime; and if he does not, he knows evil Erik will take his place, and perform the job with maximum brutality. Imagine Sven decides to do whatever has the best consequences. What happens?

Sven looks at the two options in front of him – join the police, or leave the job to Erik – and thinks through what the consequences of each of these options would be.

This is where the first problem arises, albeit a rather small one. Sven will have to imagine the police service with him in it – an image he doesn't much like – and then imagine the police service with Erik – an even worse image. Nothing wrong with that, you may say – he has to consider both options to decide which is best. The problem is that thinking of both these options is distasteful to him. The thought of Erik being cruel to innocent prisoners in a torture chamber makes him feel quite sick. If Sven is trying to do whatever has the best consequences, then he shouldn't feel sick before he's even decided. If he chose at random, or was told what to do, he wouldn't have to think about Erik torturing people. So, trying to do whatever has the best consequences is self-defeating: just doing it, which involves thinking about torture, brings about some very bad consequences – namely, that Sven is haunted by bad thoughts, and is almost sick.

Perhaps this problem is like Bernard Williams' 'one thought too many' problem dismissed earlier. Sven just needs to come up with the best response; he doesn't need to go through all the difficult and distasteful images to get there. But the problem remains: sometimes the best consequences are achieved by not seeking the best consequences. Not a fatal problem, but it is a problem nonetheless.

Sven decides the best consequences will occur if he takes the job. He concludes he should try to change the system from the inside rather than let Erik be cruel. So, he takes up the position, and tries to do whatever has the best consequences in each of the cases that come before him. It leads to a bizarre series of events, and although some of Sven's responses may seem unrealistic, they all arise from his faithful pursuit of 'do whatever is best'.

On his first day in the job, Sven deals with the wreckage of a train crash in which many people die. He finds a briefcase with money inside belonging to one of the victims, and realises it was not where it ought to be. It had been taken from its owner, whose dead body lies at the front of the train, to the back of the train, near someone who was severely crippled in the accident. Sven interviews this person, and they admit they stole the briefcase just a few minutes before the disaster. Furthermore, he discovers this thief is a repeat offender – despite being punished for theft many times before, it has never dissuaded him from stealing again. Now, though, forever confined to a hospital bed, his thieving days seem finally to be over.

Should Sven prosecute the thief? He applies his maxim: do whatever's best. Sven decides the best consequences will be served by returning the briefcase to the dead passenger's family and pretending the theft never took place. A punishment wouldn't deter further crime any more than denying there was any crime at all. The thief is now too crippled to steal again. Punishing him won't achieve anything, so Sven decides the thief won't receive any sort of punishment for his crime.

Whether you think Sven did the right thing or not, you have to admit there's a problem here. By doing whatever has the best consequences, Sven is detaching punishments from crimes.

This becomes even harder when Sven has to deal with a second case: how should he punish the train driver who allowed the crash to happen? The driver admits he made a simple but fatal mistake: he accidentally pressed the 'accelerate' button instead of the 'slow down' button. An easy error – the buttons are next to each other on the train's control panel – but a blunder which caused many deaths. Now the families of the victims want revenge, and Sven decides the best way to satisfy them is to execute the driver: capital punishment will produce the greatest happiness for the greatest number of people. Using his position in the brutal regime, he fixes the train driver's trial to give the vengeful families maximum satisfaction, and instructs the judge to issue the death sentence. Sven knows this is a very severe punishment, but it does seem to have the best consequences.

Just before the train driver is due to be executed, the train driver's identical twin brother meets Sven, and asks to take his brother's place. The twin brother has a tragic mental condition which makes him want to die. Given that the train driver wants to live and the vengeful families will never know the difference, Sven decides that everybody will be better off if the innocent man is executed in the train driver's place. So, doing 'whatever is best', Sven dutifully puts the innocent twin on death row and keeps the swap secret: nobody will benefit if the truth gets out. When the execution actually takes place, it is as painful as possible: there are many vengeful relatives and only one person to suffer the pain, so the 'best consequences' demand a gruesome death.

Sven is driven to reflect on what he has done. He joined the brutal police service to make them better and tried to bring about the best consequences. But it has meant an innocent man has been executed very publicly and painfully, and a thief has been let off. Punishments have been detached from crimes, and crimes have been detached from criminals. 'Do whatever has the best consequences' has led to very odd justice indeed. Has he really improved the police service?

Sven tries to decide what to do in other situations, but he realizes that his rule, 'do whatever has the best consequences', doesn't actually offer him much advice. It doesn't tell him how to treat prisoners, how to respond to the dictator's instructions or how much to punish people. For every problem, it just tells him to 'do whatever is best', which often seems like very empty advice indeed.

Promises, fairness, freedom, human rights – even telling the truth – everything, Sven realizes, has become secondary to the overall goal of satisfying people as much as possible. If people change what they want, or if they want nasty things, then everything that used to be 'good' can slip away in an instant. Sven finds himself serving a brutal dictator, telling lies and instituting a crazy sort of justice, all because it seemed to have the best consequences. Sven has been totally corrupted. 'Do whatever has the best consequences' seems to have stripped him of his moral character. He was good when he joined the police force. Now he feels wretched. Maybe it would have been better if he had allowed Erik to take the position after all.

When we consider Sven's tragic case, we can identify seven problems with 'doing whatever has the best consequences'. The problems are these:

1. *'Doing whatever has the best consequences' can be self-defeating.* Sometimes seeking the best consequences prevents the best consequences from being found – it forces Sven to think about nasty possibilities when it would be best if he didn't have to.
2. *'Doing whatever has the best consequences' only considers future consequences, ignoring important events in the past.* This is why Sven didn't punish the thief who stole the briefcase.
3. *'Doing whatever has the best consequences' places decision-making authority in questionable hands.* If seeking 'the best consequences'

means doing whatever satisfies people, then every whim, good or bad, can sway decisions. It leaves Sven trying to satisfy the vengeful sadism of the grieving families.

4. *'Doing whatever has the best consequences' doesn't discriminate fairly between people.* Although not discriminating can be a good thing, for Sven it meant that the innocent brother was punished in the train driver's place. 'Doing whatever has the best consequences' doesn't discriminate between people when it should.

5. *Individual concerns are sacrificed to the group interest when we pursue the 'best consequences'.* Again, sacrificing individual concerns is not always bad, but for Sven it meant the twin brother's punishment was made especially painful, just because there were lots of people watching to appreciate it.

6. *Promises, fairness and telling the truth are downgraded by the 'best consequences'.* Sven found himself lying, being unfair and breaking promises much more often than he wanted to. Although there are times when these things need to be done, doing whatever has the best consequences seems to do them too often.

7. *'Do whatever has the best consequences' doesn't offer any clear rules.* When Sven looks round for moral certainty, he cannot find it: everything is a matter of satisfying people's fickle demands. This makes it hard for Sven to know what to do. At times, 'seek the best consequences' seems like a very empty sort of advice.

These are the main problems with trying to do whatever has the best consequences. There may be others but most are variants of these. There are practical problems with trying to do whatever has the best consequences too, such as trying to work out what the consequences of an action are. But these do not make the system wrong, just difficult to apply.

At the heart of 'do whatever has the best consequences' is a more fundamental problem: the basic reason for following this advice is hollow. To see this, think back to the John Stuart Mill's beguiling proof outlined in the previous chapter – the idea that because *I* want what's best for *me*, *we* should all want what's best for *us*. This logic doesn't quite work. We may all do whatever is best for each of us alone, but the second half doesn't follow. If I buy toothpaste for me, and you buy toothpaste for you, nobody is buying toothpaste for both of us. Nobody goes into a supermarket asking what the other customers want. It makes much more sense to say that, if I shop for myself, then everybody else should shop for themselves, too. 'Do what's best for me' doesn't lead to 'do what's best for everybody' at all.

'Do whatever has the best consequences' is riddled with flaws. Even the beguiling logic which seemed to make it so attractive is not really logic at all. So what should Sven do? What should we do? Is 'do whatever has the best consequences' any use as a moral compass?

6 Can We Fix It? The Pieces of the Puzzle

Is 'do whatever has the best consequences' beyond repair, or can we alter this system for making decisions to create one we can actually use? Since so many people are still making decisions based on 'do whatever has the best consequences' – all those economists, politicians, civil servants and architects – we can find clues in seeing how the they cope.

The first thing to say is that not all of the problems emerge at the same time. When a road engineer designs a road, he does not have to make promises, institute justice or decide who deserves to travel on it – he just has to build a road. 'Doing whatever has the best consequences' is already translated for the road engineer by his road-building manual – use a certain type of surface at certain times, choose the route of the road by taking certain factors into account, and so on. In other words, a road engineer follows rules, and those rules tend to produce the best consequences. Even though occasionally it will be better if he breaks those rules – for example, the road might carry slightly more traffic than normal, justifying a slightly more expensive surface which is more hard-wearing – the road engineer won't break the rule, because he just won't be thinking in that way. The road engineer follows rules for building a road; he is only loosely doing whatever has the best consequences.

This is true of most people who think they are trying to do whatever has the best consequences. Politicians and civil servants try to do what's best, but they also respect certain accepted codes of behaviour. Most of these rules are based on doing whatever has the best consequences, but the policy-makers give them a special importance. They develop 'codes of ethics' and 'standard procedures'. Like the road designer, hardly ever are politicians and civil servants just thinking about raw consequences.

The rules these people employ overcome some of the problems inherent in doing whatever has the best consequences. Rules can uphold justice and promises, and castigate lying. They stop people thinking about the problem too much, so the system for making decisions is no longer self-defeating. The rules offer much clearer advice, so people like Sven can have the moral certainty they seek. Just as people put metal rods in concrete to give it more strength, rules seem to prop up 'the best consequences' in just the right places.

Throughout much of the nineteenth century, as problems emerged with Bentham's system for making decisions, a new generation of philosophers – John Stuart Mill, Thomas H Green and Henry Sidgwick – searched for the right rules to buttress 'doing whatever had the best consequences'. Mill, for example, made rules to guarantee personal liberties, Thomas H Green lectured his pupils to remember justice and instinct when they did whatever was best, and Sidgwick tried to bring in rules for common sense. Rules made 'do whatever's best' suitable for civilized decision-making. Bentham's wild system was being domesticated.

But, inevitably, this new generation of philosophers couldn't solve all the problems. There were times when rules for personal liberties, justice, instinct and common sense weren't quite right. Rules and 'the best consequences' would pull in different directions. When this happened, they could reinvent the rule a bit – 'don't break your promises unless . . .' – but the only way they could ever really ensure their rules led to the most desirable outcome was to adopt one rule: the same rule as Sven. And then all the old problems reappeared.

Rules can still be useful, even when they don't match up exactly with the best consequences. As long as the deviation between following the rules and doing whatever is best is small, following the rules is still a useful shorthand. It's much easier to think in rules than to calculate the best consequences for every situation that arises. In most situations, people acknowledge both the rule and the need to serve the best consequences. Politicians will agonize over whether to tell the truth or tell a lie in the national interest. Both telling the truth and doing what's best seem important, and it is a delicate matter of judgement deciding which counts for more.

It is this delicate matter of judgement which is the real problem. How should people make 'delicate judgements'? There is no simple answer because there is no longer a system for making decisions. Following rules based on doing whatever has the best consequences raises the question of which rules – how do you decide between them when they clash? Unless we can answer this, we have just an arbitrary soup of edicts. We can say things like 'promises should be kept', 'fairness is important' and 'try to do what's best', but we have no serious advice for when these instructions conflict, because we cannot follow them all at the same time.

Modern politics is full of this. Politicians call for 'Better Education' (hurrah!), 'A Strong Country' (hurrah!) and 'Prosperity' (hurrah!) without explaining which they prefer when the inevitable clashes come. Any politician who talks of values and mentions more than one should explain their priorities.

There is a way of resolving these conflicts which sidesteps the 'do whatever has the best consequences' approach of Bentham and others, and puts rule-making at the centre of decision-making. When a politician has to choose between, say, telling the truth and doing what has the best consequences, he can employ a 'rule of rules'. The idea is this: you think of how the world would be if *everybody* followed a certain rule, and decide whether that brings about the best consequences. We should act so that, if everybody copied us, the world would be a better place. This formula was developed by the Prussian thinker Immanuel Kant during the Enlightenment – not so much an offshoot of Bentham's 'do whatever is best' as an alternative, parallel approach. And it still has many advocates today: it has grown into a system for making decisions almost as common as seeking the best consequences.

This certainly has much going for it. A world in which everybody keeps their promises is better than one in which everybody lies, so this 'rule of rules' certainly makes promise-keeping out to be good and lying to be bad. 'What if everybody did that?' is a question asked by legislators when they frame laws, knowing that the law they come up with will have to apply to everybody in the country.

But even Kant's 'rule of rules' has its limits. The rule 'throw a ring to someone drowning in the water' may sound appealing, but if everybody followed it they would all rush to get the flotation device and trip over each other while the person in the sea drowned. The rule could be improved upon – 'throw a ring to someone drowning in the water unless someone else is already doing it', but then we might all stand back, waiting for someone else to move first. The more we adjust the rule to get the right result, the closer it comes to 'do whatever has the best consequences', and we're back to all the old problems which made Sven's life so wretched.

So, the best that can be done to salvage 'do whatever has the best consequences' is to buttress it with a few odd rules and guidelines. Occasionally they can be broken, but only in exceptional circumstances. We are forced to adopt a hybrid system, with neither rules nor the best consequences quite at the centre of our decision-making. Sometimes we follow the rule, sometimes we look to the consequences, and it's a matter of judgement which we ought to do in each difficult situation we face.

This is the world most of us inhabit. We think it's important to seek the best consequences, but keeping promises is important too, even when following through on a promise isn't quite best. We value fairness, but also we think helping people is good too, even when it might be unfair. We have a wide range of rules and principles, some more important than others, some specific, some less so. But we have no system for deciding between them. There is no system for making decisions which can inform our delicate judgements. Ultimately, when a dilemma strikes, we have to guess, or follow our instincts or take advice and ask someone else to decide. We need to make decisions, but ultimately we don't know how.

This is serious. It means the best attempt to correct the problems with 'do whatever has the best consequences' doesn't work. The reason this problem is so serious is that this approach is used so widely. Almost everybody – including people making the most wide-reaching decisions – have a range of principles, rules and accepted procedure, and no clear way of deciding between them. We are forced to trust the judgement of those in authority, because judgement is all we have left.

This is the problem which ultimately killed off the nineteenth century attempt to repair 'do whatever's best'. The more the philosophers tried to mend the system, the more it needed to be fixed. For Bentham's decision-making system to become safe it had to become more human, with all the quirks and character flaws that entailed, which meant it was less of a system. By the time of the First World War, alongside other Enlightenment ideals consumed by that terrible conflict, 'do whatever's best' seemed broken beyond repair.

We need a more fundamental approach, and that means addressing the most fundamental problem with 'do whatever has the best consequences', namely, that there is no underlying reason to follow it. We need to establish a new basis for our decision-making. Only then can we develop a system for making decisions which avoids Sven's seven problems with 'do whatever has the best consequences'.

So, to develop our system for decision-making, we need to find the essence of right and wrong. We need to know the most basic reason to do anything at all. Only from this foundation can we develop our new system for making decisions, and we need to make sure it doesn't suffer the seven problems we have identified with the dominant system of today.

Part II

The Proof: Finding the Basis of Right and Wrong

7   The Meaning of Life

We need to go back to fundamentals. We need to find the basic reason behind everything we do. Is there a fundamental reason for doing anything at all? This is a much harder question than it may seem: finding a fundamental reason is never easy. You can look for the reason behind the reason, but somehow you can never quite find the starting point. You get out of bed to go to work; you go to work to earn money; you earn money to buy things; you buy things to eat; you eat to stay alive; you stay alive because . . . you want to?

We are looking for the meaning of life, or at least a meaning. The search to find some sort of meaning in life is one of the oldest searches people have ever undertaken. Some people claim to have found it, but they all offer different answers.

Hindus believe the meaning of life is to pursue virtue, followed by wealth, joy and liberation. The Founding Fathers in the United States implied 'life, liberty and the pursuit of happiness' were most important. Many people live as though the meaning of life was to become wealthy, while some evolutionary theorists believe the meaning of life is to spread one's genes through procreation. Hedonists just believe in having a good time.

The pessimistic German thinker Arthur Schopenhauer thought life was basically meaningless, although he said there could be some respite if people appreciated beauty. It's a view echoed by Terry Gilliam, the man behind the Monty Python film *The Meaning of Life*: he said the question, 'what is the meaning of life?' is a nonsense question because things can exist without meaning. He says it's rather like asking 'what is the meaning of yellow?' – yellow just is. Perhaps life just *is*, too.

But this is either trivial or very disappointing: we need a more fundamental answer than that. What is the purpose of your life, and my life? What should we do with them? Is there any value to them? What can we use to persuade people not to kill themselves? These questions are all slightly different, but if we can answer just one we can kick-start our search for right and wrong.

The French philosopher Blaise Pascal, who invented the first calculator in 1642, found himself in a similar situation when he tried to deduce whether or not to believe in God. Pascal decided God must be far too complicated to understand, so we could never know whether or not He existed. Nevertheless, Pascal calculated it was better to believe in God than not to, because, if God did exist, believing in him would bring eternal rewards in the afterlife and not believing in him would bring eternal damnation; if God didn't exist, then believing in him would only cost a few hours each week at church. Hence, Pascal concluded a belief in God was a sensible insurance policy against hell, just in case it existed.

There are problems with Pascal's argument – you might believe in the wrong God, making you more likely to be damned than an unbeliever. Also, God might withhold eternal salvation from people who, like Pascal, find faith through such a cynical route. Nevertheless, Pascal's argument is very creative: he mixes his lack of knowledge with pure thought to conjure up a clear reason to believe in something.

Something similar can be done in the search for the meaning of life. Just as Pascal admitted he knew nothing about God, let's assume we don't know whether or not there really is value in our lives. The meaning in life may exist or it may not, but we can define what we're looking for: let's say 'meaning' is something really worth having, or doing.

Either there is meaning in life, or there isn't. We don't know whether there is meaning in life, but we do know that *either* there is meaning in life, *or* there isn't – one of these two situations must be correct. There is no middle option between the two.

If there *is* meaning in life, then seeking meaning might actually deliver it. You might actually find something really worth having or doing.

Alternatively, if there isn't meaning in life, then it doesn't matter what you do. You could sit and watch television, or help other people or just be nasty – it doesn't matter because there's nothing at stake. It just doesn't matter. There is nothing to be lost by pursuing the meaning of life, even though no meaning can be found.

So, whether or not there really is meaning in life, it makes sense to pursue something really worth having or doing. We should pursue meaning in life, whether or not there is any true meaning to be had.

Put simply, we should *seek meaning*, or *seek value*. People should try to find something really worth having in life, whatever that may be, whether it is there to be found or not.

The meaning of life is this: to seek out something really worth having or doing.

Purists might argue this is an empty answer, or at least a circular one. It's not far from saying that the meaning of life is to try to find the meaning of life. If someone asks you where something is ('what is the location of the vacuum cleaner?'), telling them to look for it is not much help ('try to find the location of the vacuum cleaner!'). But this is not an exact analogy. The question 'what is the meaning of life?' is special, because trying to find the fundamental meaning of something is different to asking about some characteristic of it, such as where it is. Also, the question 'what is the meaning of life' is always asked by a living person, so the 'meaning of life' question refers to the questioner, giving it another odd characteristic. It's a question which refers to itself – 'what is the meaning of *my* life?' So, trying to find the meaning of life, you may be glad to hear, is not like looking for a vacuum cleaner.

If the answer we have to the meaning of life is unhelpful, then you might prefer to ask a slightly different question. Instead of 'what is the meaning of life?' consider 'is there a fundamental reason to do anything?' With this question, the logic of the answer is much clearer. Whether or not there really is a fundamental reason to do anything, there is nothing to be lost, and everything to be gained, by seeking out something really worth having or doing. So there is a fundamental reason to seek value in life. Whatever you do, seek value.

This may be excellent news to someone driven to suicide by the emptiness of life: if life *is* empty, then that is a reason to live it like there's nothing to lose! But before you rush off to seek value, there are two caveats to be aware of.

First, there might be value in life but pursuing it might make it harder to find. The best things in life often come to those who don't look for them. There are examples of this in other areas of life. Some plants grow best when you don't look after them – if you try to grow these plants well then you will fail. Some philosophers say trying to be happy can be self-defeating – you will be happier if you don't actively pursue happiness. This problem perplexed the great Victorian philosopher John Stuart Mill, a man who wanted to maximize the total amount of happiness in the world, so much that he suffered a mental breakdown. The motto 'just live!' can inspire a more fulfilling existence than 'try to find whatever makes you happy'.

This possibility doesn't undermine the case for seeking value; it just means the best way to seek value in life might not be the most obvious. If pursuing value makes value harder to find, then value should be pursued differently. So 'seek value' means do whatever makes you most likely to find something worth doing in life. You don't have to seek value directly, and you may be better off not trying to.

The second possibility is that there definitely isn't value in life. If you can be absolutely certain that there is no value in life, then there is no reason to seek value. But then, in this case, it doesn't matter anyway – there is no reason to do anything! There's not even a reason to say 'seek value' is pointless. So, even though this grim possibility exists, there is no reason to let it worry us.

So there *is* a reason to do things – seeking value makes sense. Whatever you do, seek value.

We now have the foundation we need. From this fundamental point we can construct right and wrong. We have a basic reason to do things. From this base, we can start to build up the system for making decisions we need.

8   A Plan for Robinson Crusoe

Daniel Defoe's book *Robinson Crusoe* has been incredibly popular ever since it was published in 1719. The novel tells the fictional firsthand account of an adventurer who becomes shipwrecked on an island. Crusoe has to do more than survive: he must decide what to do and what his priorities are. Several themes in the book have echoed throughout literature ever since.

Defoe was a puritan who had a clear view on how people should live, and used the Crusoe tale to offer advice: Crusoe found a Bible which transformed his life. We can use Crusoe's fictional scenario slightly differently – it offers a certain sort of test ground in which varying complicating factors, like modern society, are removed. Crusoe's relatively simple situation allows us to experiment.

We already know Crusoe should seek value – that is the meaning of life. But what exactly should he do? Before we can offer Robinson Crusoe advice, we need to interpret 'seek value'.

You can find an answer to 'seek value' through this simple test: think of something that seems really valuable – something really worth having or doing. For example, you might want to change the world, or raise a child. Then draw up a second list of things you really want. You should find the two lists are really quite similar. If there *is* something really worth having or doing, then what people want seems a reasonable place to start looking for it. After all, if you ask someone 'what do you really value?' and they answer, 'a fulfilled life and a healthy family', there is probably something in their response. Ultimately, we are always seeking something we want. So, our search for value starts with what we want. This doesn't mean value *must* lie in what we want. People can want things which aren't worth having, and there are things worth having that many people don't want. But wants and the search for value are both fundamental to how we live our lives. Finding value in life isn't exactly the same as doing what we want, but it is the best place to start looking.

By thinking about what we want ourselves, and observing what other people want, we can learn these six things:

First, different people want different things. Although there are some common patterns (everybody wants water and shelter), everybody's set of wants is unique.

Second, our wants are created in several ways: by our circumstances, our genes and by outside influences. The experiences people have can influence what they want. But even though our wants have different origins, most still feel like 'our' wants. Knowing your want for sex can be explained through evolution, for example, doesn't make you want sex any less. Advertising may inspire you to want something, but it's still you that wants it. It is difficult to disown a want, whatever its source: wants belong to the people who have them.

Third, we can influence which wants we have. People can actively steer themselves to want certain things. We can acquire tastes for certain foods, or certain positions at work. This isn't true of all the things people want – the want to breathe is fairly fundamental. But, if you think of all the things you want now, there's a good chance you want some of them because of a decision you took some time in the past.

Fourth, people always prefer their wants to be fulfilled rather than simply negated – that's what wanting something means. If you're waiting for a particular piece of news and someone tells it to you, it matters that they're telling the truth. A lie doesn't substitute for the real thing. Drugs and hypnosis might be able to beguile you into thinking a want has been satisfied, but they cannot provide real satisfaction.

Fifth, our wants can contradict each other. It is easy to want two or more things which you cannot have at the same time. Whenever you cannot afford to buy two things you want, you have to choose between them. When we're faced with problems like this, we make choices. We choose which want we prefer to satisfy. And this reveals there has to be something else, something more important than normal wants, which helps us choose when wants conflict.

And sixth, satisfying wants tends to involve seeking certain experiences. If you want food, then you want the experience of eating. If you want to travel, then you want the experience of going abroad, and so on. This even applies to wants directed at other people: if you want a far away disaster to end, you want the experience of knowing it is over.

The last of these observations is more complicated than it appears. Satisfying wants involves seeking certain experiences but experiences can also affect wants. Sometimes this means they cancel each other out: you want to eat, so you eat and the experience of having a snack means you're no longer hungry. But sometimes wants and experiences feed on each other – being in the city makes you want to be in the countryside, and when you are there you might want to be back in the city. Experiences can also be addictive, meaning the more you have the more you want. This means some wants can grow out of control, dominating lives and ruining them.

The circular influence of wants on experiences and back again means that if you try to satisfy your wants through experiences you can never know for certain whether or not you will succeed. The experiences you seek can affect the wants that drove you to seek them. You might develop new wants, or change your old ones in the process. You just don't know until you've had the experience, and by then you might want something different. Even if you think you're on sure ground, such as wanting water when you're thirsty, you won't know until you've actually drunk some, and by then the water will have affected what you want.

So no-one can be absolutely certain of what they really want. You can guess and you might get lucky, but you can never be completely sure. And this means that, if finding value in life comes from fulfilling wants, then no-one can be sure how to find value. If someone ever does actually find something really worth having, there has to be an element of chance in their success, because they could never have really known for certain how to find it. No-one can ever be sure how to find value in life.

There is another important conclusion: it means there is no necessary link between satisfying your wants and being happy. If you satisfy your wants, you will probably develop new ones, and with them will come new reasons to be unhappy. Most lottery winners soon want something other than money. Satisfying wants and being happy are not the same thing at all.

So, from our fairly solid foundation of 'seek value', we now have a much less certain set of instructions – it's something to do with our wants. And even though wants are so central to our lives, they are actually very complicated. Wants can conflict with each other; they can be created in ways we might not welcome, for example, by advertisers; fulfilling them doesn't always make us happy; and we need to distinguish between trivial whims and more fundamental goals. No-one can ever be absolutely sure what they really want because new wants emerge when you try to satisfy old ones. It is little wonder that people often discover they don't really know what they want.

Perhaps we can sideline all the problems that come with wants by talking about 'capabilities', or options – an approach suggested by Indian economist and Nobel Prize-winner Amartya Sen. Whatever we want, says Sen, we would always prefer more options to less, and better options to less attractive ones. But sidestepping the question like this doesn't really help us very much. If you want to know what to do today, it's not much use to know your life would be better if you had more options available to you. Having too many options may even be a distraction. You need to know what to do. Just increasing the number of options is not what you need. Increasing our capabilities is not the answer.

Are the problems with wants really so bad that they can never be solved? Our lives are driven by wants, and usually we manage to cope. For example, when we face two or more wants which contradict each other, we find a way to choose between them – we might draw on more fundamental goals, and see which want fulfils our goal better. In a similar way, we can usually distinguish between trivial wants and more fundamental ones.

Also, the problem that experiences can affect wants is not so grave after all: you look at how other people have been affected. So, even though going to university might change what you want, and you can never be sure what this change will be like, you can get a good idea by looking at someone else who has already done it. How did university change *them*? Would you like to be changed in a similar way? If you do, then go to university.

So, we can get around most of the difficulties that come with wants. We can cope when wants conflict with each other, when some wants are trivial and when wants change with experience. If we were to set out a list of instructions for someone to follow, then it would be fairly simple.

Imagine yourself stranded on a remote island again, a modern day Robinson Crusoe. Suppose you have a few things left from the ship-wreck, so you can survive for a few weeks at least. Now you have a plan! Living entirely alone, you should do the following things, in order:

1. *Seek value.* You might as well look for something really worth having or doing in life, whether it is there to be found or not. So, whatever you do, seek value.
2. *Identify the things you want.* Something really worth having or doing will probably be connected with your wants in some way. So draw up a list of the things you want.
3. *Group these wants according to the goals they serve.* To choose between wants which cannot be fulfilled at the same time, try to

cluster your wants together according to more fundamental aims. These clusters of wants are goals, or fundamental wants.

4. *Guess your most preferred goals, aware that they may change.* Choose which group of wants you think you probably like best. Try to put the different clusters of wants into order of preference. Just like wants, goals can clash with each other, and can change as people experience new things and grow older. But most people can make an educated guess at what their goals are now, and what they might be in the future.

5. *Compare your preferred goals with other people's, and with goals you may acquire in new situations.* See if anybody else has already fulfilled your top choice of goals – would you like to be that person? Experiences from other people can be used to inform your choice of goals. Having mapped out some preferred goals, both for now and in the future, these need to be checked, for example, by considering how new situations may change them.

6. *Decide which goals or situations you can and want to pursue, and pursue them.* Once you've ranked your goals and situations, a further reality check is needed: are the goals achievable? Sometimes it's good to chase an impossible goal, but not if you expect to fulfil it. When you've chosen your goals, you should follow them.

7. *Do what you want.* Some wants will have no impact on other goals or wants – generally trivial things. There is a reason to do these things, and no reason not to, so do them.

This seven-step process can go a great way to overcoming some of the problems of sorting out our wants. It can be useful in many testing situations: on a remote island like Robinson Crusoe, or in a more normal predicament, when you don't know what to do. You can repeat it as new experiences emerge, by looping back to step 2. It's not perfect, but it can help you think through your options.

However, it leaves one massive problem unresolved. Most of our deepest wants cannot be attained alone. We need other people.

The most fundamental want of someone stranded on a remote island like Robinson Crusoe is probably to escape and find company. This 'manifesto for an isolated individual' is fundamentally flawed: the individual probably doesn't want to be isolated!

And when we deal with other people, everything becomes much more complicated, as Robinson Crusoe discovered when he found cannibals on his island. As we interact our behaviour tends to affect other people's, which in turn affects whether goals will be fulfilled. This is what right and wrong is really about.

To find right and wrong, we need to know how to behave in the company of others.

9 Answering an 8-Year-Old Who Incessantly Asks 'Why?'

Have you ever wondered why you should be good? Most people take it for granted that it's good to be good, just like it's bad to be bad. You just ought to be good – that's what being good is all about. But we need more: we need to know *why* we should be good.

Without that answer we are in all sorts of trouble. For example, unless we know why we should be good, we can always be disarmed by an 8-year-old who incessantly asks 'why?' whenever we try to instruct her with words like 'should' or 'ought'. Imagine the conversation:

> 'You ought to tidy your room!'
> *'Why?'*
> 'You should tidy your room because it makes it neater!'
> *'Why should my room be neater?'*
> 'Because it makes things easier to find'
> *'Why should I make things easier to find?'*
> 'Because good girls can find things easily'
> *'Why should I be a good girl?'*

We can rebuff the child a few times, but if she persists we ultimately have only two choices. We can resort to something empty, like an appeal to our authority – 'because I say so!' – or to something circular – 'because you should!' These might stop the 8-year-old asking questions, but they cannot really answer them. Unless we know why we should be good, the 8-year-old is right to expose all uses of 'should' and 'ought' as mere authority. This was Friedrich Nietzsche's insight, which we came across in Chapter 3: he said people only use concepts like 'right', 'wrong' and 'should' to exert their power. And it's not just a problem with argumentative 8-year-olds. When the stakes are much higher – such as the decisions of a Parliament, or a decision about who gets life-saving treatment – having no proper answer to 'why be good?' is a very serious worry indeed.

The question 'why be good?' arises because it concerns relations with other people. We have already established that people should seek out something really worth having or doing in life, and for most people this involves some sort of interaction with others. Our relations with others can form the centre of our lives. When these relations go well, life can be sweet. When they go badly, life can be terrible. The way people relate to each other usually determines how much they enjoy life. So, given that we should seek value, and that much of life involves seeking good relationships with others, perhaps value emerges from these relationships. 'Seek value' soon leads us to something like 'seek good relationships'.

To make relationships work well, we need guidelines. A set of rules – a moral code – which tells people how to behave can make people work together better. For relations to yield their full value, people need to follow these rules – rules for good, social behaviour. It's like driving: there are fewer crashes if people obey the rules of the road. This is where 'right' and 'wrong' come in. 'Right' and 'wrong' label certain sorts of behaviour. Behaviour which follows the rules is labelled 'right' or 'good'. Behaviour which breaks them is labelled 'wrong' or 'bad'.

But this doesn't help determine what the rules should be. Knowing that right and wrong are labels doesn't tell us what is right and what is wrong. Also, if there are guidelines or rules which tell people how to behave, why follow them? What's wrong with being bad? Why not cheat? Did you ever put litter in the bin when people were looking, but drop it on the ground when you were alone? Why not be a rogue who pretends to follow the rules when really you are just being selfish?

This is an ancient problem, and one which has unsettled many attempts to propagate moral codes through the centuries. The Scottish philosopher David Hume pinpointed it most precisely when he said 'reason is a slave of the passions': people can agree to the most logical, beautiful and reasonable moral code, but what they actually do will always be determined by what they fancy. There is no automatic connection between Right and the whims which actually direct us.

Various efforts have been made to close the gap, the most famous of which came from the eighteenth-century Prussian philosopher Immanuel Kant. Kant tried to prove that people should act if they were following rules they wanted everyone to follow. He tried to show people were somehow illogical or mad if they didn't, but Kant's brilliant reasoning still couldn't quite make people do things. He could never provide the vital compulsive kick.

There are other compulsive kicks which can connect people's actions with a set of rules, indeed a brief survey of ideologies reveals several of them. Communists have used terror; Nazis have used indoctrination; nationalists have used social conditioning; the Church has used fear of eternal damnation; and nowadays jihadists use sexual desire to recruit suicide bombers with the lure of a hundred virgins in heaven. Fortunately, there are more benign reasons why people should follow a set of rules – here are three:

First, other people might punish you if they find out you've broken the rules. Someone who pretends to be nice but who is exposed as selfish can soon become unpopular. If cheating is penalized, then acting selfishly is no longer self-serving. Even selfish people will find themselves better off following the rules, so fear of punishment will provide the compulsive kick to align action with the rules.

Second, cheating might expose you to charges of hypocrisy. If the 8-year-old has said she prefers to have her room clean, then she can appear very silly if she disagrees with the act of cleaning it (although she may say someone else should do the work!). Note that there is no automatic link between saying something is good and doing it. Instead, the compulsive kick comes from fear of embarrassment, the fear of being exposed as a hypocrite which will erode your respect and your capacity to persuade others in turn.

The third reason why cheating might not work is that it is often self-defeating. Selectively following a rule – for example, only following a rule to be nice to others when people are watching – can actually be quite difficult. Children who have been asked to do an unpleasant chore, like the 8-year-old tidying her room, sometimes try to work only when they are being supervised. When their parent turns away, they stop. But they soon learn that checking whether their parents are watching can be as much of a chore as the chore they were trying to avoid. Eventually, most children accept that they just have to get on with the job. It is often easier just to follow rules than to look for ways around them.

This third reason is the most optimistic because it can be habit form-ing. It means people follow rules because they are used to following rules, and they even enjoy being good to other people. People learn to like helping others. If it's a sort of warm interaction people want, following the rules can help make it happen. Just as being allowed to play most sports requires an agreement that the rules will be followed, both to play and to actually enjoy the game, so too with human com-pany: the rules are there not just to ensure fair play but to make the relationships fulfilling. Most people want fulfilling relationships, so most people follow the rules, even when the rules aren't enforced very effectively.

So, seeking value with others usually involves being good (whatever 'being good' involves – we will come to that later). There are strong reasons to follow the rules of good behaviour: you may really enjoy being good and get a kick out of being nice to others. If you don't, then you risk being punished or being shamed as a hypocrite.

But, although it may be difficult to cheat, there seems to be no inherent reason why breaking the rules won't work from time to time.

Think of any rule: a national law, an etiquette or a rule at school. Whatever the rule, there is usually someone who tries to break it every now and again. Rule-breakers don't have to be mad, or ignorant of the rule they are breaking, indeed they can be very sane and sensible. They can be hypocritical and just not care. Usually they just think they can break the rule and get away with it. They just follow their own rules instead. Criminals who have broken laws sometimes claim the law didn't apply to them somehow – either because they didn't agree with it, or because they thought it was acceptable to exploit flaws in the way it was enforced. Some criminals treat laws like a game: rewards if you get away with it, penalties if you get caught. Not just the habitual offender, like the career burglar who admits 'it's a fair cop' when he is finally caught by the police, but also more widespread crime. Many people disrespect minor traffic laws, for instance – we park in places we are not supposed to, and *know* we are not supposed to. If we get a parking ticket or a fine, we grudgingly accept we ought to pay it. This is an example of people willingly and deliberately breaking codes for good behaviour. It is as though we were following a slightly different code of conduct, one which sees no problem with minor traffic offences as long as we don't hurt anyone and are not found out.

So people do break obvious moral codes, and frequently. Either their position is justified because they are simply following a different code – a different set of rules for how to behave. Or they cheat somehow because they put their own interests above those of other people, and lack the compulsive kick needed to bring their words and deeds into line.

So, to keep potential criminals within the law, and to answer the incessant 8-year-old who keeps asking 'why be good?', we need two things. First, we need a convincing argument why one set of rules for being good is better than another. And second, we need a good compulsive kick to make people act on it.

10 I Say This, You Say That – Can We Ever Know Who's Right?

When our television screens broadcast a story of some horrendous practice in a far-away country, we may be outraged. We may demand our politicians do something – send in the troops and stamp out this atrocity! But should we still interfere if this practice is part of a long-standing social custom? We say one thing, the village elders say another – can we ever know who's right? Should we send in our troops, or nod respectively at their local traditions?

This problem can emerge whenever people disagree about right and wrong. It is a common problem because there are so many different moral codes. Some allow people to be killed in certain circumstances, some permit multiple marriages, and so on. We cannot follow all of these codes at the same time, so we are forced to make a decision: we need to decide whose version of right and wrong should come out on top. If you say one thing is right and I say the opposite, we need to know whose version of right and wrong should prevail.

Some of the disagreement about what is right derives from disagreement about what right and wrong relate to. 'Right' and 'wrong' are labels for certain sorts of behaviour, but behaviour can mean several things. There are three broad schools of opinion on this. Perhaps the oldest view comes from the ancient Greek philosopher Aristotle, who argued right and wrong are about characteristics – virtues and vices. If you are a generous person – the sort of person who helps people cross the road, for example – then this makes you virtuous. Sometimes virtues and vices can be difficult to distinguish: too much generosity can indicate a flawed character. This can make it hard to know exactly which characteristics are virtues and which are vices.

The second opinion says 'right' and 'wrong' depend on what people do – their actions. So, helping someone cross a road is right because it is a good action; laughing at someone who can't cross without help is bad. Kant is now the most famous proponent of this view, although it has much older roots in the many religions which dictate acts – commandments – people should and shouldn't perform. Again, this view is not as simple as it sounds: if 'helping someone cross a road' is good, then various caveats and conditions need to be added – 'help someone across a road, but not if it enables them to rob a bank, and not if there's someone else who you need to save from drowning', and so on. Deciding what actions are right and wrong can be as hard as distinguishing virtues from vices.

The third opinion is that 'right' and 'wrong' should label behaviour according to its consequences – a theory which became popular during the Enlightenment, promoted by people like Jeremy Bentham and John Stuart Mill. So, whether helping a person across a road is good or not depends on the outcome. If it leaves everybody better off – the person wanted to cross the road, and they weren't going to rob a bank – then it's probably a good thing. But this view can also be difficult. For a start, there are all the difficulties identified by Sven, who followed an extreme version of this view in Chapter 5. These do not apply to all systems of right and wrong which judge behaviour by its consequences, but they can be hard to avoid. And there are always the practical problems: what *are* the consequences of your behaviour? Even deciding what an action *is* can be difficult: when Gavrilo Princip pulled a trigger in Sarajevo in 1914, was he killing Archduke Ferdinand, starting the First World War, or ruining the twentieth century? It's hard to know everything that will happen.

(There is also a fourth school of opinion – people who don't think right or wrong relate to anything. These are the sceptics, and we'll deal with them in Chapter 14).

Knowing which of these schools of opinion is correct is not easy. Different viewpoints come to the fore in different situations. When we are young, we are often told it is important to be kind to our brothers and sisters, to be brave when we have a minor cut in our knee, and so on: virtues and vices dominate and we use a character-based idea of good and bad. Then, at school, we hear about strict rules. Certain actions are right and others wrong: this is the province of rule-based ethics. Then, later still, for example, when we are part of a committee deciding which course of action our organization should take, we look first at the consequences of each option. This is the realm of consequence-based choices.

But situations don't always tell us which view is correct. Criminal law would seem to be the province of rule-based right and wrong. Illegal acts are just those: acts. But when law courts come to decide whether or not someone is guilty, an effective lawyer might try to highlight a defendant's good character, or make an excuse based on the consequences of the illegal act – 'he had to steal the money to pay for a vital medical operation'. It seems the three systems of right and wrong can cross over. They can even merge into each other sometimes. The boundaries between them are not as certain as they first appear.

This is progress, but it still doesn't solve our problem: if I say one thing is right, and you say something different, how do we resolve the impasse? Saying one of us is thinking in terms of consequences, and the other is thinking in terms of good character or rules might explain the difference of opinion, but it doesn't settle it.

To understand this problem more, consider this example. Suppose a Christian fundamentalist wants to keep Sunday as a special day. He wants people to work less on a Sunday, spend time with their family, and so on. Then he meets an Islamist who thinks Fridays are special, and wants for Fridays roughly the same as what the Christian wants for Sundays. Should the Christian respect Islam and honour both days equally – or can he ignore the Islamist?

If the Christian fundamentalist fully respects the Islamist opinion and sincerely says 'yes, Friday is as important as Sunday', then he must also bow to Jewish demands to respect a Saturday Sabbath, too. The same applies to any advocates he meets for Monday, Tuesday, Wednesday and Thursday. All days of the week can be special too, and if all days are special, then no days are really special. By respecting the Islamist's views on Friday, the Christian fundamentalist would neutralize his own faith-based view. Alternatively, if the Christian fundamentalist doesn't respect the Islamist views on Friday, saying simply 'they're wrong – Sunday is the day to take off', then how does he know his own view is better? If the Islamist is wrong about Friday then the Christian might simply be wrong about Sunday too.

And there's not really a middle way through this problem. If the Christian respects the Islamist only a bit – he lets *them* cherish Fridays, but still attaches special importance to Sundays for himself and every-body else – then he still needs some sort of reason to stick with Sunday, otherwise he can't justify his position. And if he says each person should have their own Sabbath, then he is making all Gods personal, including his own – hardly the infinite God he wants to worship. So, when some-one says something is right or wrong, whether they respect contrary views or not, they always need a reason to back up their views.

The early twentieth-century philosopher GE Moore thought we natu-rally know what is right and wrong through some sort of innate sense of good and bad – a 'gut instinct'. He thought this 'common sense' on right and wrong, a sort of intuition, could provide the reason we need to separate right from wrong. But unfortunately bad people have intuition too. Unless you know your intuitions are better than those of someone who disagrees with you, having intuition is not enough. The Christian fundamentalist and the Islamist can both have gut instincts about differ-ent days of the week, but it doesn't make either of them right. And just as you can't refer to your gut instinct because different people have different instincts, the same applies to other possible references too.

Different people have different religions, laws and etiquette. Just referring to your own religion, law or etiquette, is not enough either.

But that doesn't mean there is no such thing as right and wrong. Some things do definitely seem wrong. There is something intrinsically 'bad' about genocide. The view genocide is 'good' just isn't as convincing. Genocide is wrong, and that's not just a matter of opinion. I could try to show genocide was wrong by referring to some sort of reason – for example, that it is outlawed by the UN Declaration of Human Rights. If the person I was trying to persuade accepted the UN Declaration, then I should be able to persuade them about genocide.

So here is the trick: we try to find a reason *that the other person can accept*. When the Christian fundamentalist talks with the Islamist, he might find out why they favour Friday, and then try to show that, in fact, those arguments actually fit Sunday better. The Islamist would try to do the same thing to him. Each needs to argue on the other person's territory.

So, if you can find a good enough reason to justify a view about right and wrong, then you can persuade people to follow it. Putting forward a view doesn't mean you have to show equal respect to rival opinions, or refuse to listen to them. But you do need a reason why your view is better than another. It's not enough just to assert a point of view, but that doesn't mean there are no viewpoints worth asserting. Viewpoints need to be justified.

So yes, one morality *can* be better than another. If I say one thing and you say another, we can know who's right by referring to a good reason for deciding between our different points of view.

This may sound like feeble progress. We have just concluded that to tell one view of right and wrong from another we need a reason. This is not much different to the position we had earlier, that our system of decision-making needs to be underpinned by a basic reason why it is the best system. But we *have* advanced. First, in the chapter on 'the meaning of life', we concluded there is a reason to try to find something really worth having or doing in life. Then, in Chapter 9, we separated the reasons why people should adhere to a moral code from the compulsive kick needed to enforce it. Now, we have a big clue about the sort of reason we need to back up a moral code: it is a reason people refer to when they are trying to convince other people of their own point of view.

Gradually, we are progressing towards the foundations of a system for making decisions – decisions about what is right and what is wrong. As we shall soon see, it is a system which will resolve the conundrums about different Sabbaths, different traditions, and different views on whether to send troops to far-away countries. We will soon be able to prove there *is* an answer, and know what that answer is.

11 Applying the Sherlock Holmes Method

Sherlock Holmes may be the greatest fictional detective of all-time. He featured in 4 novels and 56 short stories, and has been depicted in many radio, television and film adaptations over the past 100 years. The Holmes character even inspired the real-life police to rethink their crime prevention methods. The man who created the detective, Sir Arthur Conan Doyle, had set a standard for fictional entertainment to which many still aspire.

Holmes was well known for his iconic pipe and deerstalker hat, but what made him truly unique was his method: he would solve mysteries with just observation and logic. Holmes would observe something about a crime, and then apply logic to work out what that observation meant. Sometimes he would spot patterns, so if a criminal had always struck in a particular way, he would gamble the next strike would have the same characteristics and act on his anticipation. At other times he would eliminate options – if the criminal had been especially agile, then certain suspects could be ruled out. These two devices enabled Holmes to work out what had happened while others, including his dependable sidekick Dr Watson, remained baffled.

What is so impressive about this method is that it can be applied with so little knowledge about the wider world. In one of the Holmes' books, *A Study in Scarlet*, the detective is described as knowing nothing about astronomy, philosophy or literature. It didn't matter.

All Holmes needed to resolve his mysteries was knowledge about the crime and a sharp mind.

Holmes' new approach to crime emerged when philosophers were approaching the world differently, too. Having lost faith with the 'do whatever has the best consequences' system and the various attempts to correct it with rules, they began studying language. In the first half of the twentieth century, philosophers like Ludwig Wittgenstein and AJ Ayer believed words didn't just convey knowledge, they shaped what knowledge could be. In the words of the colourful French writer Jacques Derrida, 'there is nothing but the text!' This meant 'right' and 'wrong' could be discovered by thinking about how people used those words. If Holmes needed nothing more than a crime scene to find a culprit, then a statement that something is right may be enough to know what right is.

So, in the tradition of both Holmes and the early twentieth-century philosophers, we will now use specimens of right and wrong to look for patterns and eliminate possibilities. Here are five statements of right and wrong – the equivalent of the crime scene for Sherlock Holmes:

'Tidying your room is the right thing to do.'
'Whatever you say about the dictator, he was right to increase taxes.'
'It's wrong that you give so little to charity.'
'John should lie to his mother – telling her the truth would be wrong.'
'Sven was wrong to punish the twin brother.'

We need to deduce what do all these 'right and wrong' sentences have in common.

First, they all provide some sort of motivation. Hearing something is right gives you a reason to do it (assuming you take the person who says it seriously). This motive to act can apply to us, or to other people. It can apply before or after an act has been done: saying the dictator was right to increase taxes is like offering the dictator a motive to increase taxes after he has done it. This doesn't mean you always feel compelled to do what's right – the motive might be squeezed out by other concerns. But if you genuinely think something is right, then that provides a motive.

We can be sure right and wrong are about motivation. Here's why: if someone tried to suggest right and wrong *doesn't* motivate, then they wouldn't be able to motivate you to disagree with the statement 'right and wrong motivate'! They could say 'right and wrong don't motivate', but they couldn't then say, '*so don't believe that* "right and wrong motivate"'. The best they could do would be to shrug their shoulders, and remain indifferent. So the assertion that right and wrong provides a motivation is unarguable.

The second thing Sherlock Holmes would say about the statements of right and wrong is that they should be consistent with themselves in any given situation. They need to be coherent. The sentence 'John should lie to his mother' becomes incoherent if it is immediately fol-lowed by 'and he should not lie to his mother'. John can't do both and neither can we.

Again, we can be sure of this, too. It would be impossible to follow a moral code which told you to do two opposite things at the same time. The code wouldn't be able to motivate you to do either, and if it can't motivate, then, as we've just seen, it's not a very good moral code. The set of rules for right and wrong would undermine itself.

This is important because it means identical situations require identi-cal verdicts of right and wrong. If you say 'John should lie to his mother', then you accept you would lie to John's mother too, if you were in exactly the same situation as him. If you don't think you should lie, then you need to be able to show how your situation is different to John's; otherwise you are incoherent. The contemporary philosophy professor Simon Blackburn has issued a challenge to anyone who can argue con-vincingly of two identical situations that one is right and one is wrong without highlighting a significant difference between them. Blackburn's challenge will probably never be met: identical situations have to yield identical verdicts of right and wrong. This will have important consequences later.

The third thing we can work out from the statements of right and wrong is that they tend to motivate people in different ways and in different amounts. This is because we all have different views about what's important, and statements of right and wrong must chime in with this to have an effect. This, in turn, means being told something is 'right' when you are very sure it is wrong is not persuasive. A set of rules for right and wrong that diverged so much from someone's instincts that it threatened the person's motive to be moral in the first place would be impossible to follow – it would neutralize the 'compulsive kick' which connected it with actions. Again, if it did, the moral code could not motivate. Statements of right and wrong must be reasonably close to our instincts to motivate us, and they can only ever motivate us so far.

So, using the Sherlock Holmes method, we have managed to work out three things about statements of right and wrong. These statements should:

1. motivate;
2. provide motivations which do not contradict themselves; and
3. be reasonably close to our instincts if they are to motivate us, and they can only ever motivate us so far.

If Holmes were with us now, he would say these three conclusions immediately highlight a problem: most people's instincts are slightly contradictory in one way or another. Many people think killing is bad but that eating meat is fine. This means there is a clash between the second and third criteria: we can either follow a code for right and wrong which is internally consistent, or follow one which matches our instincts.

When this happens, we have to ask questions. For every clash, we either have to accept there is something wrong with our instincts, or we have to find a qualification to explain away the apparent inconsistency. To think killing is bad and eating meat is fine at the same time, we have to accept that eating meat is only OK if the animal died naturally. Alternatively, we might decide to change our views and become vegetarians. Exploring contradictions in our instincts like this is vital for anybody keen on doing the right thing.

Knowing that our rules for labelling behaviour right and wrong need to motivate, be consistent with each other and can only ever motivate us in line with our instincts doesn't say much about what moral codes for right and wrong actually are. We still need to know what sort of stuff right and wrong are made of. Where are right and wrong to be found? Are they like anything else we can think of?

Again, applying the Sherlock Holmes method we can work out three things, just by examining what statements of right and wrong mean.

First, right and wrong must be more than just matters of personal taste. Saying you think murder is good is not like saying you think strawberries are good. People can disagree amicably about whether or not strawberries taste nice. Someone might like them, and a friend hate them, and they could just agree to differ on the subject. It doesn't matter if two people have completely different appetites. Labels of 'right' and 'wrong' are different, because you can argue with someone about what is right and wrong. If someone thinks murder is OK, you have to disagree with them (or report them to the police). Saying something is wrong amounts to much more than saying it just seems bad to you.

Second, right and wrong must be linked with the world around us in some way. We know this because identical situations require identical prescriptions of right or wrong, so for something that was 'right' to become 'wrong' it has to change in some way – to get 'right' to become 'wrong' without a change is Blackburn's impossible challenge. To decide someone was right to commit a particular crime, you need to know something extra about it. You need to know something about *that* crime to make it different from all the other crimes.

And third, although 'right' and 'wrong' must be connected to the world around us in some way, they need to reach inside people, too;

otherwise 'right' and 'wrong' cannot motivate. To check this result, imagine trying to explain to someone why they should release a friend from handcuffs. You have to appeal to some motivating factor within the friend, not the situation. You could tell him it's bad to leave someone in handcuffs, so he follows his inner motivation to do what's right. You could offer him money, so he follows his inner motivation to be rich. Even if you injected him with a special drug that made him undo handcuffs, the drug would need some inner motivation to play on. Right and wrong must connect with the compulsive kick upon which people act. There has to be something inside a person to allow them to understand a moral code.

So, statements of right and wrong are:

1. more than just matters of taste;
2. related to the world around us; and
3. connected with something inside us, too.

Right and wrong are partly inside people and partly outside – they are partly self-standing, as if they had one foot in the situation we are judging, and one foot in our brains to provide the motivation. Right and wrong are somewhere between tastes that are personal to each of us and facts in the outside world.

This shouldn't be a surprising conclusion because 'right' and 'wrong' are like other motivations. The motivation to eat a bar of chocolate, for example, relies partly on external factors, such as the presence of a bar, and partly on internal elements – a sweet tooth and an understanding that eating the chocolate will provide satisfaction. The motivation provides a connection between us and the world we live in; and to do this it needs both an internal and an external component. Wanting chocolate bars requires both components; motivations to do right and wrong require both components too.

This conclusion is not too different from that reached by many of the language-focused thinkers who came to prominence at the same time as Sherlock Holmes. Many of them agreed there was something important both outside and inside, but for them it was generally one or the other, not the link between the two. AJ Ayer, for example, concluded that we could only ever know things because they were true by definition, or because they were facts about the world – a view which left no room for knowledge of right and wrong. (One flaw with Ayer's position is that it left no room for knowledge of itself, either – if you believed it then you shouldn't believe it!) The language approach had taken a misturn somewhere, and it took philosophy several decades to recover.

By applying the Sherlock Holmes method to right and wrong – looking for patterns and eliminating possibilities – there is much more we can deduce. Now we know right and wrong and our system for making decisions must provide a motive, be consistent with itself and be broadly consistent with our instincts. It needs to be more than a matter of taste and connect our inner selves with the world around us. And we can be sure that a moral code which fits this description is better than a code which does not. Sherlock Holmes would be proud.

12 How to Become a Better Person (and Answer Aristotle)

Have you ever wondered how to become a better person at parties? A certain sort of magazine article offers to tell you how: simply fill in the questionnaire then look at your answers. Mostly 'A' means you need to talk to more people, mostly 'B' means you should try lurking in the kitchen, mostly 'C' means you need to pace yourself better, and so on. The magazine has advice for every letter you 'mostly' answered.

These questionnaires do not say As are better than Bs. Instead, they offer tailored advice for each answer. It is a modern fashion to say characteristics don't make people better or worse, only different. Indeed, this view has dominated much twentieth-century thinking: many of the philosophers who studied language believed characteristics couldn't be rated or compared. It is a view which has permeated modern culture, perhaps even defining it in the 1960s.

And it is a new view: throughout the Middle Ages, many scholars devoted countless hours deciding whether honesty was better than bravery, believing there was a clear answer to be found. To the medieval thinkers who followed Aristotle's virtue-based approach to right and wrong, questions like this were profound. Today, we might be tempted to dismiss such queries, along with 'how many angels fit on the head of a pin?' But if being good rests in having the right characteristics, then what characteristics should we have? We still need to know what are the most virtuous of virtues. Acknowledging people are different doesn't tell us how we *should* be, and that's what we need to know.

Some characteristics we can sieve out straight away. Someone may be a good driver, or writer, or dancer, but these are not virtues – they are skills. Skills just allow you to do whatever you decide to do, and they aren't directly relevant to right and wrong. The ancient Greek philosopher Socrates thought knowledge was the ultimate virtue because it allows you to strike the right balance – to be courageous without being foolhardy, and to be generous without being profligate. But even this sort of knowledge is just another skill – it's about knowing when you have reached the line, not knowing where or why the line should be drawn in the first place. What matters is the virtue which provides the motivation in the first place. It is deciding what to do that requires virtue, and that is where right and wrong come in.

Selfless behaviour usually seems virtuous. Most cultures place a high regard on people who help others without any benefit to themselves. Most people have an intuitive respect for people who are kind to others. Of course, there are times when looking after yourself is best, but being selfless seems to go to the heart of many virtues. Can we show selflessness really is what 'being good' is all about?

First of all, we can dismiss the view that selflessness – altruism – doesn't exist. People can and sometimes do act out of concern for others. Examples of genuinely selfless human behaviour are actually quite common. Most people who donate blood do so selflessly. Many real-life disaster stories tell of heroic deeds (as well as extremely selfish ones). Charities and philanthropists help people every day. Although some of this help is not really selfless – it's done to enhance reputations, or for promised benefits in the future – much of it really is entirely genuine.

There's no escape from this. The late seventeenth-century writer Thomas Hobbes, who thought human kindness was a sham, would say the blood donor *chose* to give blood, so really they were doing what they wanted. But this confuses what people want to do with what is in their interests. Selflessness exists, and when it happens, it really is selflessness.

Most selflessness is inspired by empathy. Empathy is the virtue of imagining the concerns of someone else as if they were your own. Whenever you think 'I wouldn't like to be in their situation', or 'I feel really happy for you', you are empathizing with that person. Empathy is a virtue, and it often motivates people to help others. The motivation to act on love, affection and welfare in a one-to-one situation is often an empathetic motivation – they all involve imagining the concerns of the other as if they were your own.

Obligation is a slightly different sort of motive, but it can also drive people to behave selflessly. Obligation to an imagined contract-like moral duty to other people is the force behind sentiments like 'that's something I really ought to do'. Loyalty can be the virtue of obligation by another name: people imagine a contract-like commitment to another person which motivates them to rate the interests of the other person, as well as their own.

Empathy and obligation do not guarantee someone is good. If you empathize with a bad person, or act on an obligation towards them, you might do something bad. Empathy and obligation are not enough on their own.

But empathy and obligation *are* very special sorts of virtues. They are very special because they are the only virtues which match the description we have for 'good'. They have that 'partly self-standing' quality we were looking for. When you empathize with someone you match up something internal (your motivations) with something external (their concerns). When you act on an obligation, you do the same: you match up your concerns (internal) with no other person's (external) through a sort of contract, just as motivations link your brain with the world around you. Empathy and obligation have the same DNA as right and wrong. They are the same sort of stuff.

Some other characteristics also have these qualities, but only sometimes. Normal motives, such as the desire to eat chocolate bars, for example, can be partly self-standing like empathy and obligation, but the same is true of equal and opposite motives, such as the desire to leave chocolate bars alone. For each of these normal motives there is an equal and opposite motive, so you can't use these normal motives to build a consistent set of rules for right and wrong. The same is true for shared beliefs: a common belief people should shake each other's left hand, for example, is partly self-standing, but so is the opposite belief, that people should shake their right hands, too. Empathy and obligation are special because they always have the characteristics of right and wrong, automatically and consistently, and their opposites do not. This means something rooted in empathy or obligation must have more of the essence of good about it than something which is not.

This is actually a very powerful method for dismissing all sorts of rival theories. Whenever anybody says 'you should obey this set of ideas', they should be given a test: they must show that the equal and opposite set of ideas is not viable in some way. So if they tell you to obey God, they must explain why following an imagined 'anti-God' who tells you to do the opposite doesn't make sense. Since empathy and obligation can pass this test, all other systems for providing advice must either come into line with empathy and obligation, or fail the test. Empathy and obligation set the standard; rivals must be based on them or be inferior.

So, empathy and obligation are the only basic virtues. Uniquely, they match what we know we should be looking for when we look for right and wrong. Right and wrong evolve from concern for others through empathy and obligation. All other accounts of right and wrong either restate this in different words or they are flawed.

Now we can answer the medieval followers of Aristotle who wondered whether it was better to be brave or honest: whichever involves acting on empathy or obligation. We even have something which tells us how to behave at parties.

13   The Help Principle

So empathy and obligation are the two basic ingredients for being good, but to complete the recipe we also need to know what to do with them. We need a method to convert the ingredients into advice for action.

Method was at the centre of an approach put forward by the American liberal John Rawls in the 1970s. Rawls believed people were distracted from being good by self interest. Rich people favoured tax breaks; workers were more likely to support trade unions; women were more likely than men to be feminists, and so on. If these self-interests were stripped away, Rawls thought, people would make much fairer decisions. So he imagined a situation in which people had to make decisions without knowing about themselves. Whether they were rich or poor, healthy or sick, and so on was kept secret. All they knew was that they preferred being better off to being worse off and that they were scared of taking risks. People made ignorant in this way would then be asked to agree basic principles for behaviour. Rawls said they would favour the least well off person in any situation because they would be afraid it might be them – this is Rawls' famous Difference Principle, essentially that we should 'help whoever is worst off'. He concluded other principles too, some of which will be covered later. But his key insight was method: he used an imaginary process to turn a basic idea into a principle for action. Rawls' work was a major turning point in twentieth-century thinking.

We can use a method similar to Rawls' to think through what it means to act on obligation. Like empathy, obligation is a virtue which underpins other virtues. People feel obliged to do what is right. Acting on obligation involves acting according to an imaginary contract with other people. To know more about how obligation motivates people to act, we need to explain this imaginary contract and what it tells us to do.

This imaginary contract is not like other contracts. If I owe you some money because I signed a piece of paper which says so, then that's a real contract. It could be enforced by law or threatening never to speak to me again if I don't pay up. But if I pay as promised just because I feel I ought to keep my promises, there is a more basic obligation at work. It's this fundamental obligation to keep your other, normal obligations that counts.

We need to investigate this most basic obligation. We know from Chapter 11 that this most basic obligation has to be partly self-standing – it can't be an obligation only one person feels; it has to be shared in some way. This means the imaginary contract must be between two people, and if one person breaks it the other is less obliged to stick to it also.

If people could convert this most basic obligation into a written contract, what would they want the contract to say?

If two people can make a contract and expect to honour it, we can work out three things. We know:

1. both people must be capable of applying and understanding the contract;
2. they must have some concerns of their own (otherwise they have nothing to gain, nothing at stake through making the contract); and
3. they must be capable of being concerned about the other person (otherwise, they would not expect to honour the contract – they could just break the agreement whenever it suited them).

This allows us to work out two more things: since these three things apply to everybody making the contract, the same is known about both people who sign it. The imaginary contract must give the same obligations to both parties. So:

4. one person's basic moral obligation to another must be the same as that person's basic moral obligation to them; and
5. people's basic obligations from the imaginary contract must remain unchanged even if they swapped places.

But this is all we know. We don't know their particular circumstances, so we don't know who is richer or most talented. We don't know what they like or want, and unlike Rawls, we don't know whether or not these people are scared of taking risks.

Now imagine you and I are drawing up an imaginary moral contract. All we know about ourselves is the five facts listed above, and we need to decide what principle we agree on. We could test several principles to see whether they match up. What we are looking for is a basic moral obligation which both of us want and which remains unchanged when we swap places.

Three possibilities will fail the test straight away. We would reject the laissez-faire 'Don't help the other person at all' because one of us is likely to appreciate help from the other and it may be very easy to give. We would reject the egalitarian 'Help the other person until you both have the same' because it would probably involve bringing one person down more than it brought the other person up. And we would reject Rawls' Difference Principle 'help whoever is worst off' because people don't need to dislike risk to write a contract – gamblers can write contracts too, so there is no reason for us to err towards Rawls' Difference Principle.

We might consider the so-called Golden Rule – 'Do unto other as you would have them do unto you', which has been advocated by many religious figures all over the world. This certainly comes close but it's still not quite right. The Golden Rule would be bad if it turned out one of us liked being harmed. If I enjoyed being kicked, then the 'Golden Rule' would suggest I should kick people so that I am kicked in return. Some fanatics have no aversion to death: the 'Golden Rule' might inspire them to kill others in suicide missions – the 'Golden Rule' is dangerous in the wrong hands. Although it captures something important, it's certainly not the best principle to adopt.

Of all the principles we could test with the five basic conditions, the one which would come out best is this: *Help someone if your help is worth more to them than it is to you.* This is the basic Help Principle. It means each of us would offer help to the other if they needed it, but not if that help was too difficult to give or if the help would be wasted. Like triage, the Help Principle ensures help is directed where it can do most good. The Help Principle will encourage you to give money to someone who needs charity but not so much that you need charity yourself. It means trying to rescue a drowning man, but not making a pointless sacrifice that causes you both to die. We will discuss it more soon.

'Help' in this context does not just mean emergency assistance – it means doing anything which is valuable to either of you. And since seeking value is what life is about, this advice can apply to almost everything people do.

Of course, there is always the chance that one of us would break this imaginary contract – after all, it's only imaginary. We feel our obligations towards others but that doesn't mean we always act on them. What if one of us *did* break the contract? There is never a fundamental justification for lying or breaking an agreement. Try to think of an example – all viable justifications for lying or contract-breaking require some justification *other* than lying or contract-breaking itself. If it's justified then there will be an excuse. You can never break a contract just because it's right to break contracts – thinking that way betrays a big misunderstanding of what contracts actually are. So, any obligation to break a promise is not really a fundamental moral obligation. This means we can exclude it from our thinking, at this stage at least. Lying and breaking promises are dealt with in later chapters.

We can check this result by thinking through what it means to act on empathy. When you empathize with someone, you imagine their concerns as if they were your own. Their concerns are given equal status to yours. Empathy does not mean abandoning your own concerns for those of another; it means treating your concerns and their concerns the same. So when you act on empathy towards someone, you try to do whatever's best for both of you. You will help them as long as you don't lose out more than they gain. Empathy says you should help another person as long as your help is worth more to the other than it is to you. This is the basic Help Principle, again: *Help someone if your help is worth more to them than it is to you.*

You may – or may not – be surprised to notice empathy and obligation both lead to the same principle. This is because both require showing as much respect for another as for oneself. Empathy does this through a special imaginative link with the other person; obligation does it through imaginary rules. In some ways, empathy and obligation are interchangeable: sometimes you empathize with people because you feel obliged to; sometimes you feel an obligation to empathize with them. But they are distinct reasons to do what's right, even though they both point firmly in the same direction: towards the Help Principle.

So, now we know what being good is all about. We should help people if our help is worth more to them than it is to ourselves. This is the basic Help Principle, and it should guide our actions.

14 The DNA of Right and Wrong

It's now time for a very grand claim: we have found the essence of being good. More than that, we can underpin a comprehensive system for decision-making. We have the ultimate justification for what we do.

As with all grand claims, we need to be careful. Is it really this easy? Many philosophers have suggested it's impossible to get this far. Others have come up with some nasty problems which we still need to deal with. So, this chapter will check what we have done. We will retrace our thoughts and consider the inevitable attacks.

First, a summary of our conclusions so far. We have deduced we should all seek value – we should all look for something really worth having or doing. And because most really valuable things involve other people and it's easier to interact within a framework of accepted behaviour, seeking value means we need a system of right and wrong. People have different opinions about what these rules for right and wrong should be, but that doesn't mean that no view is best – one view *can* be better than another as long as there is a good reason for it.

To find this reason, we have looked into what 'right' and 'wrong' mean. Right and wrong motivate, and to motivate, they need three other characteristics: they must offer consistent advice for identical situations (you cannot follow contradictory advice); they must be broadly consistent with people's instincts to be moral (you cannot follow advice which steers away too radically from what you already believe); and, like all motivations, right and wrong must be partly self-standing, which requires being partly inside people, and partly outside, so they can connect your thoughts with the world around you. Since a moral code has to motivate, it needs to have all these characteristics. A moral code with all these characteristics is better than one that is missing one or more. These characteristics help us locate the DNA of right and wrong.

To find a match to this DNA, we looked first at characteristics – virtues and vices. Here we found empathy and obligation provide a unique match; no other virtues or vices matched up nearly so well. So empathy and obligation are the basic virtues. They are what being good is all about. When you act on empathy and obligation, you act on the Help Principle – you help someone if your help is worth more to them than it is to you. If you act on the Help Principle, then there is something essentially good in what you do. So here we have it: being good means acting on empathy, obligation and the Help Principle. That's what good is.

So that's the theory. Now, we need to check it, and test it against the various problems and attacks.

First, the problem of 'characteristics, actions or consequences' we came across in Chapter 10: is being good about having the right virtues, doing the right things or making good things happen? The answer is: all three. Empathy and obligation are good characteristics. The Help Principle is a guideline for good action. And if you act on the Help Principle, you will be considering consequences. 'Right' and 'wrong' are a bit like light, which behaves like waves in some experiments, and more like particles in others. Whether it's better to think in terms of characteristics, actions or consequences depends on the circumstances. The basis for 'right' and 'wrong' transcends all three categories.

Second, we have to answer the sceptics. There are several of these. Thomas Hobbes and Friedrich Nietzsche, both of whom had a depressing view of humankind, thought right and wrong were just a mirage which disguised selfishness. Other sceptics, such as the twentieth-century Australian John Mackie, claim the terms 'right' and 'wrong' can't refer to what we think they refer to, so using them automatically involves error. Some sceptics say there is no reason to do anything at all.

We can take the sting out of these objections enough to stop worrying about them. There *is* a reason to do something, because there is nothing to lose by seeking value, whether it is there to be found or not. 'Right' and 'wrong' don't refer to anything solid or tangible, but they are useful labels which motivate us to behave in certain ways, just like red and green traffic lights tell us usefully whether to stop or drive on. 'Right' and 'wrong' are not just disguises for selfish persuasion; they involve a serious degree of selflessness, and selflessness we can prove to exist. These responses could be more detailed, but suffice to say that there are responses, and they are reasonably robust.

Also, some of the sceptic arguments undermine themselves – if you take them seriously, then you're forced *not* to take them seriously! A statement that says 'don't do what's right because it's all an empty deception' can be discounted as an empty deception itself. Sceptical statements like this can't persuade someone who wants to be good to behave any differently.

Very similar to this is the surprisingly common view that right and wrong are fiction. This view is often linked to evolutionary theory – that concepts of right and wrong evolved with our species. Right and wrong may well have evolved in this way, but it doesn't take us very far. An infatuated adolescent can read an evolutionary explanation of his unfamiliar emotions, but it won't help him decide what to do. Some who hold this view do go further, and say it's good that we believe in right and wrong. We *should* teach our children right and wrong, they say, even though we're not actually teaching them anything. But this view self-destructs after a few moments' thought. If right and wrong are fictions from evolution, then how can it be 'good' that we believe in them? If we *should* teach our children right and wrong, then at least one part of right and wrong, namely that we should teach them to our children, is not fiction.

The third problem we can tackle is the 'I say this, you say that, how can we know who's right?' problem. Now we know. One person's 'right' will be better than another's if it has all the characteristics needed to motivate. We can work out a system for 'right' and 'wrong' and know it is better than other systems. If I say this and you say that, we can compare both of our statements against the criteria for right and wrong, and find out which of us is correct.

Fourth, we can deal with a religious fundamentalist who tells us to do certain things 'because God demands it'. For every such command, there is an equal and opposite command which we can attribute to an anti-God, who has their own book of (un)holy words. Fundamentalists must pass this challenge: they must explain to someone who is neutral on the matter why their God is better than the anti-God without locating 'good' in some Godly virtue, such as love, that could be followed in its own right. Fundamentalists should be more worried than they will be that this challenge is impossible. However, we *can* answer this challenge for empathy and obligation: they automatically and consistently have the tell-tale characteristics of right and wrong while their opposites do not. This test suggests there is more reason to act on empathy and our obligations to other people than to obey God.

Now for some problems we've not come across yet. The great Scottish philosopher David Hume showed 'right' and 'wrong' cannot be pinned down by drawing on observations. He said you cannot study the world around you and, from those observations alone, decide how it should be. Put simply, Hume said you cannot go from an 'is' in it to an 'ought': 'he *is* stealing' cannot lead to 'he *ought* not to steal' unless you already know stealing is wrong. If Hume were alive today, he might wonder if this is what we have done.

Fortunately, we can escape this objection because we've done something slightly different. We haven't looked at how the world is. We've looked, instead, with the Sherlock Holmes' method, at 'right' and 'wrong'. They're not in the world like normal objects; they're motivations. We've not gone from an 'is' to an 'ought', but from an 'ought' to another 'ought'. Lots of people use words like 'ought', 'good' and 'right' – we've just tried to find the best way to use those words, for example, by making sure you don't use two 'oughts' which contradict each other. And Hume would find nothing wrong with that.

Another problem arises from the question, raised by the Cambridge professor GE Moore in the 1930s, 'Are empathy and obligation really the best basic virtues?' The problem is the very fact it's a reasonable question, an open question for which the answer might be 'no', which means empathy and obligation don't quite define 'good'. Moore argued that if we think of 'virtue' and 'good' in a different way than 'empathy' and 'obligation', then there is a problem – there might be a way to do what's right without empathy or obligation.

Now we can answer GE Moore's so-called 'open question' argument, based on work provided by his contemporary successor at Cambridge, Simon Blackburn. To see if empathy and obligation could diverge from right and good, we need to assess them. It's difficult to assess a virtue other than by another virtue, which requires testing that virtue against another virtue, and so on. To escape the circle of assessing virtues by other virtues, there needs to be some other way to assess them. Since we now know good is a partly self-standing motive, then whether a virtue is a partly self-standing motive seems to be a fair measure. And by this measure, it's not an open question whether empathy and obligation measure up. The reasonable question, 'Are empathy and obligation really the best basic virtues?' is not open any more – it's answered. Empathy and obligation really *are* what being good is about.

Finally, we need the compulsive kick to make this account of right and wrong connect through to people's actions. We have three. First, for people who get a kick out of helping others, this philosophy motivates through the joy of acting on empathy. Second, for people who are driven to improve the world, we can prove the Help Principle is the best way to make the world a better place. And third, for people who assert rival theories, there is the 8-year-old with her incessant question. By asking 'why?' she can trace back any system of right and wrong to show either it is this system by another name, or it involves a contradiction, or it has no more appeal than the equal and opposite theory. So if you don't follow this account of right and wrong you risk being shamed by an 8-year-old, and that shame can provide a very compulsive kick indeed!

So we *do* have the DNA of right and wrong, and the basis for a system of decision-making. It still needs to be refined as we shall see, but the difficulties with it are problems of interpretation and practicality, not with the system itself. The challenge now is to build it up into a workable system: a system that offers sound advice, a system to help us understand what 'good' is, and a system which can make the world a better place.

Part III

The Principle: Refining the Help Principle

15   Putting the DNA in a Petri Dish

Help someone if your help is worth more to them than it is to you.

This is the basic Help Principle, the essence of right and wrong – the DNA of good, if you like, made from a double helix of empathy and obligation. Now we need to grow this DNA into a complete life-form, something able to advise us in all our decisions.

The strategy will be to nurture this basic essence into the working system through an organic process of refinement and redefinition. Like a scientist putting a living organism in a Petri dish (a Petri dish is a small, plastic container with nutrients at the bottom that enable the organism to grow), we will see how empathy, obligation and the basic Help Principle can be expanded into the system for making decisions we need.

Cultivating right and wrong in this way is not new: Rawls, the American, tried something similar in the 1970s. He called it 'reflective equilibrium' – he would test notions of right and wrong against his own intuitions, then reflect on which needed to be changed. Sometimes he had to revise his theories of right and wrong; sometimes he had to adjust his intuitions. This way he could bring his intuitions and ideas into line and gradually expand the range of affairs he covered. His system had the virtue of producing coherent principles of right and wrong which were suitable for many situations. The problem was that these were essentially the intuitions he started with. Unlike Rawls, we will start with the DNA of right and wrong, and only use intuition to alert us when we have seriously gone wrong. The challenge is to find knots in the DNA and untangle them, not to justify our prejudices.

To see how far we have come and how far we still need to go, think back to Sven and his efforts to do whatever was best in the police state. His system for making decisions, do whatever has the best consequences, had seven problems with it.

Doing whatever has the best consequences:

1. can be self-defeating;
2. only considers future consequences, ignoring important events in the past;
3. places decision-making authority in questionable hands;
4. doesn't discriminate fairly between people;
5. sacrifices individual concerns to the group interest;
6. downgrades promises, fairness and telling the truth; and
7. doesn't offer any clear rules.

How many of those problems does the basic Help Principle share, and how many does it manage to avoid? Alas, it shares too many: the basic Help Principle is little more than 'do whatever has the best consequences' applied to just two people. To see how much the Principle needs to be refined, consider this example.

You are a master locksmith. Walking home late at night, you come across four people looking very suspicious. They seem to be trying to unlock the door of a house and you recognize one of their faces as a man wanted for a string of local burglaries. As a lock expert you can help the burglars break into the house, or you can walk on pretending not to notice them and swiftly call the police when you get round the corner. What should you do?

The answer seems obvious – the burglars should be reported to the police, not helped to commit another crime. But if you apply the basic Help Principle, you will compare the cost of the help you can offer to them – a few seconds delay, and a little queasiness – with the value of your help to them – whatever they can steal from the house. If their plunder is worth more than your few seconds delay, then the basic Help Principle seems to advise you to help the burglars!

The basic Help Principle shares several of the flaws inherent in Sven's system for making decisions, 'do whatever's best'. To see which ones, we need to consider each problem in turn:

1. *'Doing whatever has the best consequences' can be self-defeating.* The basic Help Principle can be self-defeating too: the basic Help Principle still says you should help people like the burglars, even though they may be intent on stopping the Principle be applied.

2. *'Doing whatever has the best consequences' only considers future consequences, ignoring important events in the past.* Unfortunately, the basic Help Principle also considers only the future consequences of helping people. It ignores what the burglars have done in the past and we end up helping someone with a very bad track record, someone who does not deserve to be helped. We need to refine the Principle to remove this problem.

3. *'Doing whatever has the best consequences' places decision-making authority in questionable hands.* The basic Help Principle shares this problem too – the burglars have very questionable hands but we help them just the same. This needs to be tackled.

4. *'Doing whatever has the best consequences' doesn't discriminate fairly between people.* The Help Principle is OK here. Whereas Sven saw no difference between the train driver and his innocent twin brother, the Help Principle involves one-to-one relationships between you and each of the four burglars. If they had different needs, you could cope with each of them individually. This problem has been addressed.

5. *Individual concerns are sacrificed to the group interest when we pursue the 'best consequences'.* The basic Help Principle only operates between pairs of people – between you and one other. Would it make a difference if there were eight burglars, or sixteen? The basic Help Principle has a blind spot here. We need to find out how to apply the Help Principle to groups.

6. *Promises, fairness and telling the truth are downgraded by the 'best consequences'.* The basic Help Principle has nothing to say about

these, but it seems to fall into the same trap as Sven's rule: you end up helping burglars, not the householder. We need to apply the Help Principle to things like promises more clearly.

7. *'Do whatever has the best consequences' doesn't offer any clear rules.* The basic Help Principle offers one clear rule – itself! But we need more than that. We need rules to tell us what to do in a whole range of situations, and we need to make sure they don't conflict with each other. And, of course, we need rules which stop us helping burglars!

So, the basic Help Principle manages to avoid only one of the problems that come with 'do whatever has the best consequences'; the other six it shares or does not yet answer convincingly. We need to cultivate the Principle so it has none of them.

This third part, from here until Chapter 22, refines the Help Principle to answer most of these problems. The general tactic is to identify each problem in turn, then refer back to the roots of right and wrong – empathy and obligation – to find the answer we need. You can skip straight to Chapter 22 if you just want to see the results of this process rather than the process itself. But if you want to know *why* some things are right and wrong, then turn the page.

16 Using Your Watch to Tell Right from Wrong

Imagine this:

You advertise for someone to fix the wiring in your home. It's an expert job that needs two days of skilled work. A qualified electrician responds to your advert and agrees to do the work for the going rate. The electrician works diligently and, at the end of the second day, he's finished. The electrician did the work reasonably well and he was motivated by the fee you promised him beforehand.

Should this electrician be paid? The obvious answer is 'yes': workers like this one, who do what is expected of them, should indeed be paid.

But suppose you apply the basic Help Principle – you decide to help the electrician by giving him money only if it is worth more to him than it is to you. What happens? On the first day, paying the electrician means he earns his fee, and you have your wiring fixed for a price you are prepared to pay. Both of you are happy. So, if you applied the Help Principle on Day 1, you would pay him. But by the end of the second day, things will be different: the work will already have been done, so the reason for paying him will have gone. The only certain consequence of paying him when he has finished his work will be to give him money. If the fee is worth less to him than it is to you, then when you apply the basic Help Principle, you wouldn't actually pay him. Of course, the electrician might refuse to work again or threaten legal action. But then again, he might decide to write off your debt or even forget your original advert promised him money. Whether or not you should pay him no longer depends on the fact you promised you would. So, according to the basic Help Principle, it's right to pay the worker on Day 1, but some time on Day 2 it's no longer right. If you knew exactly when, you could look at your watch to decide whether it's right to pay the man for his work!

This sounds absurd, but it is actually more common than you might think. Politicians often have to choose between their old election promises and what seems best for the future – usually they find a messy compromise. Judging actions only by their future consequences misses something big: it means there is no *direct* reason for honouring commitments, even though the motivation to keep our word can be as strong as the motivation to help other people. It seems to be a fundamental part of what 'right' and 'wrong' are about. The idea that actions can be judged solely by the consequences which come after them is also unrealistic: people cannot be motivated solely by the future consequences of their actions. People just don't think like that. We don't just look forwards in time when we make decisions – we always look backwards, too.

We need to find out how time fits together with right and wrong. We need to know how are they connected, and justify our intuition that you can't tell right from wrong by telling the time.

Time is rather mysterious. If we looked for time we probably wouldn't find it. We might not even know what we are looking for. But time seems to affect the world around us. It makes us feel older. Things change over time, and it's the change we notice.

This means time is something to do with the world around us. We already know, from David Hume, that you cannot tell right from wrong just by looking at the way the world is. Even with obvious crimes, like murder, witnessing the crime is not enough to know it is wrong – you cannot condemn an act of murder unless you know murder is bad. Witnessing murder and knowing the time are both observations about the world. Neither of them is enough to tell you right from wrong. So, if an action remains identical in every respect (the overall circumstances, the character and intentions of the people involved, what they did and the consequences, etc.) except that it happens at a different time, then whether that act is right or wrong will not change. There can never be a moral difference between identical acts carried out at different times – they are identical, so whether they are right or wrong will remain the same, too. We need to look away from our clocks to know what we should do.

Physicists tell us time is very similar to space, so they should have similar relations with right and wrong. If two acts are carried out in different places but remain identical in every other respect, we wouldn't expect one to be right and the other to be wrong, they must both be right or both be wrong. As long as two acts are identical, when they happen matters no more than where they take place.

But the similarity between space and time also shows there can be a sort of link with right and wrong. If I fire a rifle vertically into the air, then I can expect the bullet to land somewhere within about 50 metres of where I am standing. If I'm very unlucky, it will land on my head and kill me! If there are other people within a 50 metre radius when I fire, then they could be killed by the falling bullet, and firing the gun would be highly irresponsible. It doesn't matter where I fire the gun – the rightness or wrongness of pulling the trigger does not depend on where I stand. But it does depend on whether other people are nearby when I fire. So, right and wrong are independent of space and distance, but space and distance *as they affect the nature of the action* do matter.

So too with time. It doesn't matter *when* I fire the gun. Firing the gun at midnight is the same as firing at noon if I am alone on both occasions. But it does matter if there are people nearby when I fire. If I wait a few minutes to allow some bystanders to walk away, then that makes me slightly better because it makes the people safer. Waiting for people to leave before I fire the gun is a good thing to do.

It's this notion of time we need to incorporate into the Help Principle. We need to make the Help Principle sensitive to time changes which affect the nature of an action, but insensitive to time changes which do not. There are a few ways in which time can affect the nature of an action, such as when it's bad to be late: time determines whether someone is late, so time will determine whether or not they are bad, too. Time can affect attitudes and attitudes can affect the nature of an action. It might be right to apologize immediately after you committed a faux pas, but an apology several weeks later would be out of place. Time also affects *us*. We can only remember things from the past, not the future; we can only change the future, not the past; and we can't understand actions before living memory in the same way as contemporary ones. Consequences beyond human foresight are just too far away to think about. Time *does* matter.

In all these cases, a time element changes the action, and this change can affect whether or not the action is right: time can *indirectly* affect what is right. But the link between time and what is right can only ever be indirect. It's not the time itself that is making something right or wrong, but the way time affects something else, and its that something else which is influencing whether it is right or wrong.

So does this mean the electrician gets paid?

The electrician will work as long as he expects to be paid, so the time you actually hand over the money will not affect what he does. If you tell someone you're going to do something and they plan accordingly then you have some responsibility for what they have done. This is why it's right you pay the electrician. The Help Principle must become insensitive to when you pay him.

If the electrician had known he wasn't going to be paid before he started working, then he wouldn't have worked. This is a 'past consequence' of paying the worker. These imaginary past consequences are the changes in behaviour that have already happened in the past because the act was already known. The imaginary past consequence of holding back the electrician's fee would be that he wouldn't have done the work.

Because what is right doesn't depend directly on time, these imaginary past consequences should have the same importance as normal, future consequences. When the two sets of consequences – past and future – are combined, it is like making a decision about when to pay the electrician before he does the work and sticking to it. We can call this the 'all-time' consequences of an action. The all-time consequence is the difference an action makes whenever that difference happens. These differences can occur *before* the action because people can form reasonable expectations about what you are going to do and act on those expectations beforehand – you promise the electrician a fee, so he does the work; you promise a toy to a child, so he gets excited; you promise someone a meal, so she doesn't cook one herself, and so on. When actions are judged by their consequences, we cannot just consider effects that happen after we act; we should consider the all-time consequences.

Applying this to the Help Principle, it is the 'all-time' value of help that counts. So, if your help is worth more to someone else in the future than it is to you, then they should be helped. But also, if you already promised to help them in a particular way, and this made them do things differently, then that provides a reason to help them too.

This means the basic Help Principle needs to be refined. Instead of simply 'Help someone if your help is worth more to them than it is to you', it now becomes: *Help someone if the* all-time value *of your help is worth more to them than it is to you.*

And yes, you should pay the electrician.

17   Letting People Choose for Themselves

If you type in the words 'voluntary' and 'death' into an internet search engine, you will be confronted by some very tragic personal stories. People like the 38-year-old woman with degenerative Huntingdon's disease who wants to 'do something' about the amount she will suffer before her inevitable decline. People like the 28-year-old man with terminal cancer who believes death is the only satisfactory cure to his intense pain. People like the parents of a teenager who died horribly from disease because he was not allowed to end his life as he wished.

Should we help these people to die?

Different situations warrant different forms of help. A child wants attention; a bankrupt wants money; someone drowning at sea wants to be rescued, and so on. The most appropriate form of help clearly depends on circumstances. So, if someone is suffering terrible and terminal pain, switching off their life-support machine could be a tremendous help to them.

We usually think of 'help' in quite narrow terms – giving money to poor people or emergency aid in times of crisis – but we need to think much wider. Almost everything we do impacts on other people, so almost everything is a potential form of help to others.

If someone offered you help right now, what would you ask for? Most people have a good idea – we usually know what will benefit us the most. Not always – there are plenty of examples of people making mistakes about what is good for them, becoming addicted to something nasty, making bad decisions in a bad mood or taking unsuitable advice. But these are the exceptions. We usually know what is good for us because we have spent so much of our lives learning. Through trial and error, we are permanently sifting what we like from what we don't. Finding out what is good for us is one of our central concerns.

In other words, we are all naturally tuned to doing what's best for ourselves. Only when something knocks us off balance is this not the case. We can be off balance because we don't know something special – an option which seems attractive is really much worse than it appears because we lack some rare piece of information. We might be too young to form a proper judgement about something, or our ability to understand a situation might be clouded in some way – by alcohol or depression, for example. Since most people get it right most of the time, it is reasonable to assume they can make appropriate decisions for themselves unless we *know* the person lacks expert knowledge, that they're too young to understand, or that some temporary condition is hindering their judgement.

This argument was used by the great Victorian philosopher, John Stuart Mill, the man who tried to prove people should do whatever had the best consequences. Mill argued that because people tended to know what was best for them, they should be free to do whatever they want as long as they didn't harm others. This freedom, Mill thought, would enable people to develop both themselves and the world around them. Mill's idea that a decision should usually be made by the person most affected by it is now widely regarded as common sense. We should listen to the people we are helping because they will usually be best placed to decide the best sort of help they need. The helper may have an idea too, but unless they know something special, the recipient is likely to know more about what's best for them.

Involving people in the process of choosing their own help also makes people more attached to what they get. Much international

development work emphasizes the need for participation by the bene-
ficiaries of aid.

Put this together, and you have what we can call the 'Autonomy
Principle' – the idea that the person receiving help should usually be
involved in choosing what help they receive. We should *let people
choose for themselves, unless we know their interests better than they
can.* This Autonomy Principle is a good general guide when deciding
how to treat people.

How can you know someone's interests better than they do? Many
people assume they know best as often as they are wrong. To really
know someone else's interests better than them you must be able to
see a chink in their judgement they cannot see themself. You need a
clear reason why they cannot know what's best for them, a reason they
would accept if they could.

There are some limits to everybody's autonomy. Our minds are limited, which means there is only so much we can consider before we
choose: we can compare five products before we buy but not five hundred. We can't know everything about everything which may affect us.
Sometimes this means someone else has to step in to ensure some
basic standards, such as safety requirements on complex pieces of
equipment. But this shouldn't reduce people's autonomy. We need to
empathize with people who don't have the time to make a conscious
decision about things, and we also need to empathize with people
whose decisions may differ from the majority.

So, if a person wants to die, should you help them?

When the sort of help someone wants is irreversible, is major or is
not what you would want for yourself, you need to be particularly careful. These three conditions increase the chances of giving the wrong
sort of help or that your 'help' is very damaging, and with requests for
assisted suicide all these three conditions would apply. You would have
to triple-check that they really did want to die, that they had thought it
through properly, and so on. You should empathize with them to
understand their alternatives, to imagine the misery of a painful

terminal illness. You would want your judgement of these things to be confirmed by other people, probably experts, and people who know the person making the request. You might want to pause for several days or weeks to make sure the person's thoughts were not a passing psychological condition, and that there was not some better option both of you had missed. But, if the person really did want to end their life, and they fully understood all this meant, then you should indeed help them.

The distressing personal testimonies on the internet are real, and we should respect these people's wishes. Autonomy is often the only thing these people have left and we should not take it from them. In these extreme cases, and under heavily regulated conditions, voluntary euthanasia is the right thing to do – you *should* help them die.

18   Torturers and Charitable Show-Offs

Erik likes to watch people being tortured. He has a cruel fascination with watching others suffer pain. While other people collect stamps or watch football, Erik studies new methods of inflicting agony. Should we let him?

Most people say 'no': torture is a very bad thing and we ought to stop it whenever we can. But can we be so certain? Most people at one time in their lives, perhaps when they were children, have laughed at someone else's distress. Violent sports are very popular. In a cruel world, gaining pleasure from the displeasure of others is widespread. Erik's love of seeing others in pain creates a problem for the basic Help Principle because it means we could 'help' people by harming others for their amusement.

For an example of 'helping' people by harming others, imagine you are sitting with a very immature friend in a busy café, and an over-worked waitress is approaching down the aisle. The waitress is carrying a big pile of dirty crockery, and she cannot see where she is going. You can easily stick out your leg and trip her up – she would fall, and her plates and cups would smash all over the floor causing great amuse-ment to your juvenile companion. This amusement is worth much more to your friend than sticking out your leg is to you. You may be deeply ashamed, but that's nothing compared to the fits of giggles your friend would enjoy for many weeks. Like Erik, he gains pleasure from the misery of others, so your help is worth more to him than it is to you.

The Help Principle seems to advocate tripping up the waitress! Something seems badly wrong.

This is a very similar problem to the dilemma posed earlier, when you met the burglars. You can help the burglars enter the property and your help is worth more to them than it is to you, but it will be very bad for the home-owner being burgled.

Erik who enjoys watching torture, your immature friend in the café and the burglars pose a special problem for the Help Principle. All of them want your help, but that help entails being nasty to an innocent person. Acting on empathy with the innocent person requires the opposite. In other words, these cases seem to make the Help Principle contradict the empathy on which it is based.

This is a problem caused by particular sorts of want – 'person-to-person' wants. These are wants someone has for someone else. Person-to-person wants can be good – wanting well of others; bad – wanting them to suffer; or specific, such as wanting them to do a specific thing, like trip up and spill their crockery. Person-to-person wants are a problem because they invite us to act according to the opinion of others rather than the value to the recipient. If people really appreciate watching someone being tortured, then this can 'outweigh' the torture victim's pain. If enough people enjoy watching her fall, then why not trip up the waitress?

The problem is not just with bad person-to-person wants, like enjoying watching people suffer. Even good person-to-person wants are difficult because they work against everybody else, everybody for whom you *don't* have a good person-to-person want. If you go into a famine-ridden refugee camp, for example, and you act on a good person-to-person want to help a particular person, it means you will make a special effort to help them survive. Better than helping no-one, you may say. But it means you will be helping that person for the wrong reasons; they may even be the wrong person to help. It means deciding who gets food on the basis of what makes *you* feel good rather than who needs food the most. Your person-to-person want that somebody is healthy will mean other people go hungry. So acting on 'good' person-to-person wants can be as cruel and selfish as acting on bad ones. All person-to-person wants make us choose for reasons other than the right one, which is how people can be helped.

Can we ignore these 'person-to-person' wants when we apply the Help Principle? Most of us feel sorry for the waitress, we would be happy for torture to be outlawed and we want the refugees to be treated fairly. Our instincts drive us towards excluding these 'person-to-person' wants as much as we can. But can we justify excluding them with anything more than our intuitions?

We can find the answer by looking at the twin roots of the Help Principle – the virtues of empathy and obligation.

Acting on empathy towards a person involves imagining their concerns as if they were your own. It involves stepping inside someone's head, seeing what they want and considering it important; other people's person-to-person wants are out of the picture. When you empathize with me, what other people think of me is something separate. It's not in my head, which means it won't be in your head either when you imagine you are me. So, according to the empathy derivation of the Help Principle, we should ignore person-to-person wants.

When the Help Principle is derived from obligation, it is drawn up like a contract: an imaginary contract between two people who know only limited information about themselves and each other. Like any contract, people who have not signed it cannot be bound by it, and people who sign the contract cannot be bound by those who have not signed. So the contract gives us every reason to ignore person-to-person wants. The obligation derivation would also exclude person-to-person wants when the Help Principle is applied.

So, when we apply the Help Principle, we should only count value people derive from objects. Any value people derive from other people – seeing them do well, or badly – is excluded, because we treat those people separately.

A new concept is needed: 'direct' value. 'Direct' value means value derived from person-to-object relationships; it excludes value from what people want for others. This tightens the Help Principle. It now becomes: *Help someone if the all-time* direct *value of your help to them is greater for them than it is for you.* Put another way, the person-to-person wants of others should have no direct effect on how you treat a person. As an instruction, this means: *Do not treat people by the wants of another.* People should be treated according to their own wants and intentions, not by what others want of them.

This maxim was laid down by Kant more than two centuries ago when he argued that people should always be treated as 'ends', never as 'means'. Totalitarian regimes which terrorize ten people to encourage a thousand to work harder would have horrified him, as they probably horrify us. It is wrong, Kant would have said, to treat the ten by the wants of the others; the ten must be treated as those ten individuals deserve.

Unfortunately, ignoring what people want of others leads to some uncomfortable conclusions. People's relationships with other people often seem more important than people's relationships with objects, and for many people they are the most important thing in their lives. Just think of the doting grandparent, or the adoring spouse: these people have person-to-person wants at the centre of their universe.

Since the Help Principle is based on the person-to-person virtues of empathy and obligation, excluding person-to-person wants from the Help Principle may even be self-defeating. It seems to eliminate the main motives to act on the Help Principle. And if a system of right and wrong undermines the basic motive for us to follow it, it cannot motivate us to do anything. We seem to have struck a very big problem indeed. But this line of thinking is only half right. The Help Principle is not excluding *all* person-to-person wants. The full Help Principle, 'Help someone if the all-time direct value of your help is worth more to them than it is to you', is actually codifying person-to-person wants based on empathy and obligation. It just applies these directly to people, and excludes other ways of applying them to avoid double-counting. It is as if the Help Principle is assuming you want well of others, and then acting on that assumption. Whether you really want to help the waitress or trip her up, the Help Principle assumes you want to help her. The Help Principle only undermines some forms of empathy and obligation – it undermines empathizing with and forming obligations to people who have ill-intents towards others. Happily, this means excluding person-to-person wants does not make the Help Principle self-defeating after all, which is good news.

But this does have implications for how people should act.

Whenever you enjoy good things happening for others you can gain a special extra pleasure yourself. This is most obvious when we exchange gifts. Most people enjoy giving presents away. Giving can be more enjoyable than receiving. We can enjoy helping others, and we can foster this enjoyment. We can try to align our own person-to-person wants with the Help Principle, and so increase our pleasure when we do 'good' things. This means we enjoy applying the Help Principle – we gain a 'bonus benefit'. Since this 'bonus benefit' does not provide any sort of loss, only a gain (a 'bonus'), there is every reason to seek it. So: we should apply the Help Principle, and also *learn to enjoy* applying the Help Principle, so we can win a 'bonus benefit' from our good work. We should enjoy doing good things.

There is one final problem with this: the problem of the charitable show-off. We have all come across this person – someone involved in good works purely for their own ends, perhaps seeking a certain sort of reputation or place in society. These charitable show-offs seem to be involved in charity for all the wrong reasons. It is as though they've learned to enjoy applying the Help Principle a little too much.

In these cases, what matters is whether or not the Help Principle is applied; impact on person-to-person wants and bonus benefits is ignored. The charitable show-off should enjoy the bonus benefit that comes from being good; they should not be penalized for it. The principle is that we should treat people according to their own wants and intentions, not by what others want of them – it doesn't matter whether you help someone for selfish reasons; what matters is that you intend to apply the Help Principle. If someone does something good (such as help someone) but with a selfish motivation (because it will make them popular), this warns of a potential problem in the future (the person may continue to seek popularity rather than help others, when the two motivations require different actions). So don't rely on charitable show-offs when the chips are down, but there is no problem until the selfish motivation and the good actions pull in different directions.

To see how this fits with most people's intuitions, including probably your own, think about the mother of a severely disabled boy. The boy needs full-time care and attention. The mother finds his demands quite overwhelming at times even though she loves her son deeply. How much should she help him? Should she fulfil all his needs, even though it drives her beyond her limits? According to most intuitions, how much the mother should help her disabled son should depend on whether she genuinely finds the work tough. To get an exact answer, she should help him until an extra hour of help is worth less to him – because he's had enough help – than it is to her, because she really needs a break. This is the Help Principle applied. However, how much help she gives should *not* depend on whether or not she enjoys seeing him prosper. She shouldn't give him unwanted help just because she wants to, nor should she withhold help because she likes to see him suffer. This fits with the idea of excluding bonus benefits when deciding how much people should be helped.

This bonus benefit approach can be expressed as a simple maxim: *Try to enjoy providing and receiving help in line with the Help Principle.* You should enjoy helping others, and you should enjoy being helped yourself. There should be no shame in it. The caveat to be aware of is this: the desire for this enjoyment should not drive action away from the recommendations of the Help Principle. We should treat people by their own wants and intentions, not by what others want of them, as shown by Kant. It is what a person wants and needs for themselves that should count first and last when you decide what to do for them. We should make other people happy and enjoy doing it, but not if, like Erik, their happiness depends on the misery of others.

19   Revenge, Reciprocity and Received Wisdom

Driving along you see two cars broken down on the roadside. You slow down, and realize that standing frustrated beside each one is a person you know. One is kind and generous, the other is selfish. As you draw in and park your vehicle, they both call across to you for your help. Naturally, your instincts lead you to help the kind person first. But should you really?

Selfish people try to receive help without providing it in return. These are the rogues we discussed earlier – people who cheat the rules, making it harder for society to function. Selfish people stand to benefit from people who apply the Help Principle without having to sacrifice anything themselves. Selfishness is a danger: if a few people get away with this then others may be tempted to copy them. A trickle can become a trend, and before long, nobody will be helping anybody else. The Help Principle will dissolve, perhaps taking with it the spirit of good society.

To be effective, the Help Principle needs a strategy for coping with people who do not apply it. We need to know what to do when we see a nasty person who needs our help. To find out what this strategy should be, we need to go back to the genesis of the Principle – the twin virtues of empathy and obligation.

To empathize with someone is to imagine their concerns as if they were your own. Part of this involves taking on that person's level of empathy for other people. So if you empathize with someone who doesn't themselves empathize very much, it follows that your empathy for that person will be similarly low. We should empathize with people only as much as they empathize themselves. Expressed as a rule, this is: *Apply the Help Principle to others as much as they would apply it themselves.* This is a rule based on reciprocity, the reciprocity rule.

Obligation leads in a similar direction. If we were drawing up an imaginary contract to set out our most basic obligations to each other, and we were looking for a rule which would deter each other from reneging on those obligations, then the reciprocity rule is the one we would adopt. Remember that, when we are drawing up the contract, we only know some very basic information about ourselves and each other. In those circumstances, the reciprocity rule seems to provide the best deterrent to people who might otherwise exploit the Help Principle.

The reciprocity rule draws on a recurrent theme common in many diverse codes and cultures. Socrates, the ancient Greek philosopher, said 'Do not do to others what would anger you if done to you by others.' Chinese Confusionism contains the 'Doctrine of the Mean', which includes the advice: 'One word that can serve as a principle of conduct for life [is] reciprocity. Do not impose on others what you yourself do not desire.' Brahmanism and Hinduism advise 'This is the sum of duty: Do naught unto others which would cause you pain if done to you.' Although each culture expresses it slightly differently, the idea of mirroring your treatment of others with their treatment of you is very widespread indeed. Interestingly, most of these ancient wisdoms express the reciprocity rule negatively – advice about what you should *not* do, rather about what you should. We will see why soon.

Doing to others as they do to you has been studied extensively in modern times. Various experiments have shown it is often a very successful strategy, and it is used in all sorts of real-life situations, too. Driving along at night, for example, if you see a car with its headlights raised to full beam making it harder for you to see, the best response is often to retaliate in kind: you put your headlights to full beam also.

When the other car dips its beams, you dip yours too. By the time the cars approach each other, both cars should have dipped headlights, minimizing the danger of a crash. Retaliation in kind seems to work – both in theory, and in practice.

Reciprocity is particularly important when people are attacked. When someone is attacked without provocation, it amounts to a sort of negative help – the Help Principle applied in reverse. So the reciprocity rule entitles helping them in a negative way too. This would amount, usually, to self-defence against an attack. Hence, the reciprocity rule justifies self-defence.

When the reciprocity rule is combined with empathy, it involves imagining yourself in the position of someone entitled to self-defence: if you see someone being attacked without good reason, empathy suggests you should try to defend them as you would defend yourself. So we have a moral duty not to ignore people being abused, but to try to help them. Each of us should defend people who are attacked without reason as if we were attacked ourselves. This is a sort of duty to intervene. It applies at a small scale, when we see someone suffering from minor crimes in the street, but also on an international level. The duty to intervene provides a clear obligation to get involved in dangerous situations whenever we can improve them significantly at little cost to ourselves.

But there are problems with reciprocity.

First, in one sense, simple reciprocity can *never* work. If you were to reciprocate everything that happened to you exactly and immediately, then whenever anybody gave you a birthday present, simple reciprocity would mean you had to give it straight back! With simple reciprocity, just 'do to others as they do to you', even someone helped in line with the Help Principle – a starving person offered some food – would have to return it. No-one would be able to apply the Help Principle at all. To correct this, reciprocity has to apply not to specific actions but to the intentions which inspire them. When I give you a birthday present, it's the wider description of the action that counts. So, if I picked out a special gift for you to celebrate your special day, reciprocity shouldn't mean simply handing the gift back. Reciprocity means waiting until it's my birthday, and then giving me something equally well-chosen (and so probably different).

Second, reciprocity doesn't always work. Big people pick on little people because the threat of the little person fighting back is not very scary – reciprocity provides no deterrent. Also, someone who has already been attacked in a certain way might be invulnerable to further attacks in the future. 'An eye for an eye' does not deter the blind!

Third, reciprocity can lead to an endless cycles of retribution. If I think you spilt my drink, and regard the appropriate response is to thump you, then I might launch my fist towards your chin. You, perhaps unaware that you had accidentally knocked my drink, would consider the punch unprovoked and retaliate in kind. I would punch you back, and you would retaliate again. My drink would remain spilt, fists would fly and we would accumulate bruises to no good purpose. 'An eye for an eye', as Mahatma Gandhi once lamented, 'only ends up making the whole world blind'.

In examples like these, one person applies reciprocity to another, who applies it back to the first. When it's unclear who initiated the chain of reciprocity it's unclear who should end it, and the tit-for-tat blows can swing back and forth for ages. This is exactly the reason why so many of the ancient wisdoms discussed earlier explain reciprocity in purely negative terms – advice for what you *shouldn't* do. When reciprocity becomes positive advice, explaining how much people should be punished or penalized, it becomes complicated and incendiary.

We need to know what to do to stop cycles of reciprocity. Imagine a mutual friend saw us trade punches because we disagreed about the split drink. If she empathized with me, she would realize I was simply and honestly applying the reciprocity rule as I thought it should be applied. You thought the same. Neither of us was really being nasty, so neither of us deserve to be condemned to an endless cycle of punches and punching.

Empathy suggests people should intervene to stop a cycle of reciprocity between two or more other people whenever blame is unclear. When both people sincerely believe the other is at fault and their retaliation is justified, then others have an obligation to try to make them stop their quarrel. This adds to the duty to intervene: you should *defend someone who was attacked without due reason as if you were attacked yourself, and intervene to stop a cycle of reciprocity if you can reduce the amount of undeserved harm that is inflicted.*

But what if there was no-one to intervene? Would we just keep trading blows over the spilt drink? This leads to the third problem with reciprocity: exactly *when* should you reciprocate?

We showed earlier that when actions take place doesn't affect whether they are right or wrong: you could reciprocate before or after someone does something bad – it doesn't matter. But this answer is not really convincing. If you reciprocate *before* someone does something bad, then how do you know they're going to do it? And if you reciprocate *afterwards*, then how can your reciprocity change anything? Reciprocity before an action is uncalled-for, and reciprocity after an action can be little more than spitefulness.

These thoughts, and the fear of endless cycles of reciprocity, have inspired some to abandon reciprocity altogether. Jesus is credited with the now prevalent idea of not retaliating. 'I tell you not to resist an evil person', he said, 'But whoever slaps you on your right cheek, turn the other to him also.' This has an appeal. Not retaliating at all means your attacker stays unharmed, which can be a good thing, especially if they didn't mean to harm you, or if there was a misunderstanding somewhere. Also, if your attacker has a sense of shame, inviting a further blow might discourage them from striking you again. But unfortunately most people who attack others are not nice people. If your attacker is rational, then they should understand deterrents, and reciprocity deters more than the 'threat' of not retaliating. If your attacker is not rational, then it is hard to predict the effect of making it easier for them to attack you again. If you are attacked, there are at least four options which are usually wiser than 'make it easier for your attacker to hit you next time'. These options are remove the provocation, summon help, run away and defend yourself.

Islam has a more mature view on this than Christianity. Mohammed said people could reciprocate harm done to them or their family ('there is no blame on them'), but Allah would smile on them if they didn't actually do it. Forgiving the misdeeds of others allows one's own misdeeds to be forgiven. Islam also asks people to examine the motives of people who harm others, which helps protect against endless cycles of reciprocity. Applied correctly, Islam enables people to both deter and forgive in line with the Help Principle.

Reciprocity is the backbone of deterrence, but it needs to be applied with a safety valve to prevent needless harm to others and to stop cycles of reciprocity getting out of hand. It involves measuring the situation and deciding whether you should follow through on the threat of reciprocity, or whether it's best to let it go. We will need to empathize with people who might qualify for forgiveness but they shouldn't know when to expect it. So although Chapter 24 offers some clues on this, there are good reasons why we can't define here exactly when we should forgive people.

Reciprocity always needs to be applied with extreme care: it involves limiting how much you empathize with someone, and that needs to be done very carefully indeed.

20 What if You Didn't Mean to Do It?

We're on a ship. Suddenly you fall overboard and struggle in the water. I throw you a life-jacket but, because I throw it badly, the wind catches it and the jacket blows away. Eventually someone else rescues you, but I accidentally failed to help you when the Help Principle said I should. A week later, we're on the same ship, and this time *I* fall off. Should you throw the life-jacket towards me, or let it blow away in the wind? Should you judge me by my *intention* to help you, or by the poor results of my *actions*?

'I didn't mean to do that' is a common sentiment. What we want to do and what we actually do often diverge. Factors beyond our knowledge, skill or control can skew the effect of our actions away from what we intended. Anyone who has ever tried to bake a cake and failed can taste the proof.

This creates a problem for people who want to do what's right, in particular those applying the reciprocity rule. The problem is this: do you apply the reciprocity rule according to what people did, or what they meant to do?

For the answer, we need to return to the twin virtues of empathy and obligation, the basic virtues that underpin the Help Principle. Empathizing with someone involves imagining their concerns – it involves linking in with what they *want* to happen. So empathy suggests it is my intentions that should be judged, not my actions. I *tried* to throw you the life-jacket, so now you should try to throw it to me also. The same answer emerges when we go through the obligation route. If obligations flow from an imaginary contract between two people, then each should want their intentions to be included, not their actions, since they have much more control over what they *want* to happen rather than what they actually *do*.

So it's intentions that count. *We should judge people by what they intend to make happen.* This alters the reciprocity rule slightly. It now becomes: apply the Help Principle to others as much as they *would* apply it themselves.

Judging people by their intentions also means there is no real difference between an action and a deliberate non-action that share the same outcome. Think back to the immature friend who wanted you to trip up the waitress in the cafe: you could stick your foot out to trip up the waitress, or, if your foot was already in position, you could deliberately leave it there. Even though one scenario involves you moving your foot and the other does not, there is no significant moral difference between both cases. They both involve you deliberately tripping up the waitress. If the waitress sued you in court a few weeks later, you would sound feeble if you defended yourself by saying 'I can't be held responsible for tripping up the waitress because I didn't do anything' if you knew leaving your foot where it was would trip her up. The intended outcome of an action must include all the likely results. If you intend to make something happen, then you must accept responsibility for other consequences likely to accompany it.

This overturns two traditional doctrines, both of which are widely held, many centuries old, and spread by people who should know better. The first is called the 'acts-omissions' doctrine, and it says there are some things it is OK to allow to happen, as long as we don't do them actively. This doctrine claims knowingly leaving your foot in the aisle to trip up the waitress is somehow different to sticking your foot out, even though you know both will lead to the same thing. This doctrine may be convenient, as we shall see, but it is wrong. The second, closely related, is called the 'doctrine of double effect', and is widely used in medicine: some doctors justify injecting lethal tranquillizers into very sick patients by saying they only *intend* to remove pain. That may be true, and their actions may, on balance be right, but they cannot escape responsibility for the inevitable side-effect, the death of the patient, simply because they didn't intend it. The doctors knew it would happen, just as they knew their drugs would remove pain. They cannot intend one without intending the other since they know both consequences come together. This doesn't mean administering fatal injections to patients in great pain is always wrong, but it does mean the most common excuse for it, the doctrine of double effect, is scandalously empty.

People may be ready to junk these two outdated doctrines, of acts-omissions and double effect. Judging people by what they intend to make happen probably tunes in with most people's intuitions. But now the logic now takes us beyond them – prepare to feel awkward.

First, if we can be blamed for what we haven't done as well as what we have, then our responsibilities grow much wider. The obvious limit to our responsibility disappears. There are probably lots of things we haven't done which perhaps we should have. For example, yesterday, we all deliberately spent our lunch money on ourselves (or are you an exception?). This means we did not spend it on any of the millions of starving people in the world. We can be blamed for their deaths because we deliberately chose to do something other than stop them die. By this account, we are all murderers many times over. This may make us uncomfortable. Of course, we *didn't mean* to allow people to die of starvation. But our actions betrayed us because we did something which we knew would have this effect. We could have stopped them dying, but we chose not to.

This point has been made by Peter Singer of Australia, recently described by the New Yorker magazine as 'the world's most influential philosopher'. Taking a cue from Mill and Bentham, Singer argues we should be judged by whether or not we pursue the best possible consequences. It is a line of thinking which leads naturally to blame us all for a famine if we spent our money on expensive lunches. Singer has been accused of hypocrisy because he spent a great deal of his own money on medical treatment for his mother while she was suffering from Alzheimer's disease. But it is unfair to dismiss a point purely because one person suggesting it may be a hypocrite. Singer is essentially correct that we must scrutinize our inactions as closely as we scrutinize our actions; the real weakness in this simplified version of his argument is that it plays down how hard it is to actually tackle famine many miles away with your lunch money. We will consider this issue later.

There is a second problem with judging people by their intentions. It means unforeseeable events outside someone's control should not influence how they are judged. To see what this means, think about this example. Two woodcutters in a forest are both swinging their axes to chop down a tree. Both men are a little reckless as they spin their heavy axes high into the air. Then, a small child – completely unexpectedly – runs in front of one of the woodcutters and is seriously hurt. (If you want a happy ending, then you can assume the child recovers to full health.)

Because unforeseeable events outside someone's control should not influence how people are judged, it means both woodcutters are *equally* culpable. Even though one hit the child and one did not, both are equally worthy of guilt. This is because both woodcutters had the same intentions and they were equally reckless; neither is responsible for the fact that one actually injured a child and the other didn't – they both took the same chance, and it's the chance they took that matters, not what luck made that chance become. So, judging people by what they intend to make happen means luck shouldn't influence how people are judged. We should be judged according to what we intended (or didn't take sufficient care to prevent), whether or not it actually happened.

This conclusion means guilt becomes a much more shady concept. It becomes a matter of risk and uncertainty; it loses its sting, and because it makes us all a little guilty of many things, the fear of guilt is less of a deterrent to people who do 'bad things'.

This conclusion also challenges our intuitions because it means we are not being judged for what actually happens. It will be particularly difficult to accept for someone on the receiving end: the parents of the child hit by the reckless axe are likely to be much angrier with the woodcutter who actually hit their child than with the one who did not. What matters to them is that their child was hit. For the victim, actions are likely to be more important than intentions. But we can answer the angry parents when they demand the woodcutter who hit their child is punished more severely than woodcutter with a clean axe. We ask the parents, 'why was it *that* woodcutter who hit the child?' The parents have to admit it was because of where the child ran. And who's responsible for that? The child or the parents, but not the woodcutters. The woodcutters deserve equal punishments; the parents need consoling.

There is yet another problem with judging people by their intentions. People have an incentive to pretend certain events were accidental when really they weren't. If really I want you to drown, then I might deliberately throw the life-jacket badly, to let it be caught in the wind and look like an accident. Some sort of deterrent is needed to stop people pretending their deliberate actions were accidental. Otherwise, the reciprocity rule will never apply: people will claim all the bad things they did were accidental. We need some sort of sincerity test. This is needed to measure how much intentions really did diverge from actions, or whether someone is just pretending they meant to help when in fact they did not.

We all come across this problem when we try to assess other people's character and decide how much to trust them. When someone fails to do what they intended, we would expect them to learn from their mistake and get it better next time. If someone repeatedly fails to match their intentions with their actions then this suggests something is awry. We wonder, how hard are they really trying if they keep getting it wrong?

The rule of thumb is this: people should be judged by their intentions rather than their actions, but when their intentions *repeatedly* diverge from their actions, then we would be naive to accept their professed intentions without scrutiny. Because people should be trying to match what they do with what they mean to do, bad intentions soon show through. *People's real intentions are best identified from the* pattern *of their actions.*

Also, people don't just have to learn for next time – they can often make amends straight away, by trying to compensate people who they've accidentally harmed. Offering compensation and applying the Help Principle can both indicate sincerity – the person *would* help if they could; they didn't mean to cause harm.

So, although we should judge people by their intentions, we need to be careful how we decide what those intentions are. If you fell in the water a second time, you should be less forgiving if I threw the life-jacket into the wind again. Everyone makes mistakes, but most people learn from them.

21 The New Ladder to Humility

Helping people isn't just a transaction. It is about kindness, generosity and sometimes humility. But should it be? Is helping other people with humility any better than helping people with brashness?

This question was the topic of a ladder of charity, drawn up by a Jewish theologian in the twelfth century called Moses Maimonides. Maimonides examined help to others, 'tzedakah' as he called it, and ranked different forms into eight levels. The lowest form of help involved giving grudgingly and immodestly. Help improves, moving up the ladder, if it is given anonymously, and if the benefactor does not know the recipient. Help given without a request is even higher up the ladder. The highest form of help, according to Maimonides, is to form a partnership with the person in need, strengthening them on a sustained basis until they are self-sufficient. By Maimonides' analysis, a blood donor who donates anonymously, not knowing who she is helping and not expecting any sort of commendation for her efforts is giving a much better *quality* of help than someone who reluctantly puts money in a tin rattled in front of her to be rewarded with an 'I gave money to charity' sticker.

Maimonides' ladder seems to rise above the crude Help Principle, which just compares the value of help between two people, donor and recipient. Modesty, anonymity and all the other important qualities identified by Maimonides seem to be ignored. We need to know whether the Help Principle and Maimonides' ladder can be reconciled.

The answer emerges from a slightly odd phenomenon: when you apply the Help Principle, you change the situation you are in. Imagine I have lots of potatoes and you are very hungry. Both of us apply the Principle to each other. The Help Principle says I should give some of my potatoes away, because each one will be worth much more to you than it is to me. So, I give you a potato, then another, and another, and so on. As I give you more and more potatoes, each extra potato will be worth less to you as you become less hungry (generally, the more you have of something, the less valuable you find each item of it to be). At the same time, as I give my potatoes away, my remaining potatoes will become more precious to me. After a time, I might be in danger of becoming hungry myself. Eventually, the next potato I'm about to give away will be worth about the same to you as to me, at which point the Help Principle no longer applies, and I should stop giving them away. Giving away potatoes once reduces the case for giving away more potatoes because each remaining potato becomes more valuable to me and less valuable to you. Applying the Help Principle changes the relationship between two people and reduces the case for applying it again in the future.

If we help each other in line with the Help Principle but fail to complete the full process, one or other of us may feel our generosity had not been reciprocated. If I gave away lots of potatoes but didn't receive much in return, I might feel that somehow I had been cheated. If I then applied the reciprocity rule, I might stop being so generous to you. The whole process of exchanging help between us could stall. There are a few reasons why this might happen. People often want to reciprocate help, but are simply unable to – someone who loses everything in a natural disaster may have no means of repaying her rescuers. Some acts of generosity are almost impossible to reciprocate: if you save my life, for example, then I am very unlikely to be able to pay you back in full. Generally, large and indivisible donations are the hardest to repay.

There is a way round this: when people cannot reciprocate help, they can usually express gratitude. Someone can show they mean to reciprocate help, whether they actually can offer help through the Help Principle in return or not. Because we should apply the Help Principle to others as much as they would apply it themselves (the reciprocity rule), it follows that everybody should express sincere thanks for the help they receive. And because people should be judged by what they intend to make happen, it follows that providing help which cannot be reciprocated licenses no sense of moral superiority. The famine victim *would* do something in return if they could, so the person who helps them cannot claim to be any better than them. Only if someone who receives help *wilfully chooses not to apply the Help Principle in return* does a moral difference arise.

So, we should *help others with humility. Providing help does not licence any sense or display of superiority, unless the recipient wilfully chooses not to return the kindness.*

Comfortingly, this broadly confirms Maimonides' conclusion (although it is not identical to it). Both Maimonides and the Help Principle agree assistance is better if it is given voluntarily rather than grudgingly, and the best form of help involves the benefactor empathizing with the recipient to provide long-term sustenance until the recipient is self-sufficient. The Help Principle calls for people to help others with humility; Maimonides concurs by ranking anonymous help above overt assistance.

Both Maimonides and the Help Principle also tackle a related problem, common in the world today. Some people only help others with a selfish caveat: they only support people who can assist them achieve their own goals. Their help to others is self-serving, not empathetic. The Help Principle deals with this through the reciprocity rule: if someone adds a selfish caveat to the Help Principle, such as 'Help someone if your help is worth more to them than it is to you, *and only if they are sufficiently powerful to help you in the future*', then the reciprocity rule entitles the same caveat to be applied to them. Someone who helps others selectively, hoping to win reciprocal advantages, will not deserve much help in return. Maimonides dealt with it by placing this sort of help on the lowest rung of his ladder of charity.

The real measure of genuine kindness is how much you help people who cannot help you in return. *How much you help people who cannot help you is the clearest measure of how much help you really deserve yourself.*

22 The First Nine Principles of Right and Wrong

We have refined the Help Principle. From the basic Help Principle, 'Help someone if your help is worth more to them than it is to you', we now have the full version, which takes account of when actions are done and the problem of person-to-person wants. And we have extended it into six other Principles for right and wrong. From the DNA of right and wrong, we now have seven basic life-forms. To these, we can add our original edicts about seeking value, empathy and obligation, giving us nine Principles in all.

These are the first nine Principles of right and wrong:

1. *Seek value.* Something worth having or doing may be there to be found, and if not, seeking it loses us nothing.
2. *Empathize, and be true to your obligations.* We have seen how any viable framework of right and wrong needs to be rooted in empathy and obligation. So to seek value effectively we need to empathize and be true to our obligations.
3. *Help someone if your help is worth more to them than it is to you.* In our fully refined Help Principle it is the all-time direct value of help that matters. The words 'all-time' are important: your actions can bring benefits before they happen because people can anticipate them, and these benefits need to be considered. Person-to-person wants are ignored; only value derived *directly* from how someone interacts with objects is counted.

4. *Treat people according to their own wants and intentions, not by what others want of them.* This means you should treat people directly, not by the wants of another, as shown in Chapter 18. It incorporates Kant's maxim that people must only ever be treated as ends, never as means to other people's pleasure.
5. *Let people choose for themselves, unless you know their interests better than they can.* This is the Autonomy Principle from Chapter 17. It draws on John Stuart Mill's work about letting people make decisions for themselves.
6. *Apply the Help Principle to others as much as they would apply it themselves.* This is the reciprocity rule, explained in Chapter 19.
7. *Defend someone who was attacked without due reason as if you were attacked yourself.* This is the duty to intervene, also from Chapter 19. It includes the duty to intervene to stop a cycle of reciprocity if you can reduce the amount of undeserved harm people inflict. We should not stand by while bad things happen.
8. *Try to enjoy providing and receiving help in line with the Help Principle.* This is the bonus benefit rule, derived from the Help Principle in Chapter 18.
9. *Help others with humility and express gratitude for help you receive.* This is the humility rule, developed in Chapter 20. Providing help can only ever licence a sense or display of superiority if the recipient of your help wilfully chooses not to return the kindness. Linking in with writings by Maimonides, the Help Principle shows the clearest measure of how much help you really deserve yourself is how much you help people who cannot help you in return.

Five out of these nine Principles might seem to be about just help, but this is misleading: 'help' needs a very wide interpretation. It includes anything which affects people including emotional support, information and new experiences. Indeed, just about everything we do is covered by it. What really matters is the all-time value of your efforts: the impact of your actions, plus any impact before you act because someone formed a reasonable expectation of what you would do. At times, helping someone might involve deliberately withdrawing other forms of help, forcing them to look after themselves. If withholding help for a day gives someone skills that will benefit them for many years, then it might well be the best thing to do.

These nine basic Principles of right and wrong are important, but we need to know more. Some situations require special thought, and it is to those situations we will now turn.

Part IV

The Programme: Extending the Principles to Other Problems

23 The Myth of Blame

On a busy weekday morning, a man in a bank queue suddenly draws out a pistol and fires into the air. A very loud 'bang' reverberates through the building. The bullet hits the ceiling, and bits of plaster flake off and flutter to the ground. The man with the gun shouts that everybody should stay still and everybody obeys. Then he demands to speak to the manager, who emerges after a few seconds, nervous and reluctant. The manager confirms he really is the manager. 'Good', says the bank robber. 'Now open the safe, and bring me all the money you have, or I'll shoot one of your customers!' The bank manager wonders whether the man is bluffing, but judges from the mad look in his eyes that he isn't. So, promptly and efficiently, the manager opens the vault and brings three large sacks to the gunman, saying there is no more money in the bank. The robber takes the sacks, orders everybody to lie down on the floor, fires again into the ceiling for effect, and runs out of the building.

A few days later the bank robber is arrested and the case comes to court. There are plenty of witnesses. The man's image is clearly visible on the bank's security cameras. The police recover the money from his flat. All the evidence says he's guilty. The bank robber intended to rob the bank, and, as we have already established, it is intentions that count. So the bank robber is to blame, right?

Unfortunately, convicting the bank robber is actually quite complicated. It's because the world is more confusing than it seems: when people should be blamed for things is not straightforward at all. The problem with convicting the bank robber is many hundreds of years old and has confounded many brilliant thinkers. David Hume, the sceptical Scot, probably framed it most clearly; he showed it is a problem rooted in how we think the world functions. Here is Hume's thinking applied to the bank robbery.

We naturally assume what happens is determined by causes having effects on things. But if we believe in cause and effect, then the robber can claim his behaviour was caused by things outside his control. Evolution *caused* him to want certain things, he says, and his upbringing in a poor neighbourhood turned him to crime. The robber's lawyer might be able to find professors who will testify that genes and upbringing are completely responsible for our character. And, says the lawyer, if we are driven by some combination of our genes and our circumstances, then it's those factors, not the robber himself, which is responsible for stealing the money.

This argument is discomforting. It gives criminals nearly universal licence. Can we respond? Whether or not we cause events, we certainly feel like we are part of the decision-causing process. We make things happen: the jury will decide on their verdict, even if they just apply predetermined rules. Indeed, you cannot make sense of a world where you cannot influence anything at all. So we could say that, even though genes and upbringing cause how we behave, this doesn't count as an excuse, because *we* cause how we behave, too. An outside influence doesn't allow responsibility to be passed up from the person doing the action to whatever influenced them – we are still responsible for our actions.

The trouble with this answer is that it puts the blame on the bank manager! After all, it was the manager who opened the safe and took out the money, so it was him who robbed the bank. The man holding the gun was – like genes and upbringing – a bad influence on the bank manager. If the man with the gun can't excuse his behaviour because of bad influences, then the bank manager can't either.

So we have a dilemma. If we trace responsibility back to whatever influences us, then criminals can blame their genes and upbringing and the bank robber goes free. Alternatively, if we say we *are* responsible for our actions, dismissing the 'genes and upbringing' alibi, then we go against the idea events have causes, we can't understand how we interact with the world, and we can't accept 'acting under duress' as an excuse. Either way, we can't hold the bank robber responsible for his behaviour without also convicting the manager. This is called 'Hume's fork': our easy view of the world is punctured whichever prong we choose.

There are three ways out of this conundrum. All three mean the bank robber ends up behind bars and the bank manager does not, but all are a little bit sly.

The first escape route is to accept that how we think has been determined by evolution and our environment acting over thousands of years. But we can still convict the bank robber and let the manager walk free because that is the way we do things. Perhaps we are not 'free' to think anything else. It is an idea implied by Winston Churchill who, when asked whether he believed his extraordinary life was determined by fate or free will, replied rather cheekily that they were the same thing. Although this line of thinking is neat, it involves a massive contradiction and doesn't really answer the problem.

The second possibility is to say our brains are unique. They might have a special ability to originate events without a prior cause, so our brains can be responsible for things because there is nothing else to blame. The bank robber pointed the gun at the bank manager, and that's that! The trouble with this is it requires an explanation of how the brain does this. How did the bank robber manage to escape his evolutionary influences? How does the brain 'magic' thoughts out of nothing? Science may soon be able to explain this, but until it does, we should not put too much weight on this approach. It is convenient, but we have no reason to think it is correct.

The final answer to the conundrum is to say this: the lack of sense either way allows a *sort* of choice to be made as to whether or not we have responsibility. No sense will be lost whichever decision we take. Whether or not people have responsibility for their actions, things are much better if we assume they are. People generally do consider the likely consequences of an action when they decide whether or not to do it, and it is a good thing they do.

This seems like an odd move. We can help people by telling them all sorts of things but it doesn't make them true. The point here, though, is different. We can't make sense of whether or not we really are responsible for our actions. We just can't understand it either way. So, what we decide on the matter isn't true or false – it's nonsense either way. All we have left is to choose which sort of nonsense we prefer, and we might as well choose the sort of nonsense that the Help Principle endorses. It's like choosing the most useful map there is to guide you through unchartable territory.

This approach owes much to William James, who pioneered American pragmatism about one hundred years ago. James and others were annoyed with academics who posed clever problems without solutions – they wanted ideas to have what they called 'cash value'. Pragmatists like James argued it was OK to believe something if it worked. Hence, William James argued it was OK to believe the bank robber was responsible for robbing the bank because this was a useful way to think. Indeed, he tried to prove his position was correct by declaring 'I chose to believe in free will' noting that 'choosing' *not* to believe in free will was not possible. James took the idea a little too far, into the realm of wishful thinking. But we don't need to follow his view to the extreme to hold the bank robber responsible for the crime: we can blame the bank robber as long as there is no alternative way of thinking which makes more sense.

Of course, that doesn't mean that we are responsible for everything. The bank manager who took the money from his safe because a gun was pointed at a customer was clearly acting under duress. Making him responsible won't achieve any good. We only need to hold people responsible for their actions *as far as they could choose between the likely consequences*. This let's off the bank manager; but it means the bank robber *is* responsible. He wasn't forced to rob the bank; he chose to commit a crime, so he's guilty. If he tells the jury he was brought up in a rough neighbourhood it won't qualify as an excuse.

So we *are* responsible for our actions. *We are responsible for our actions as far as the likely consequences can influence our intentions.* Finally, we can convict the bank robber.

This explanation of responsibility doesn't just answer the conundrum of convicting the bank robber. When you think through what it actually means, it also explodes the modern myth of blame. This is the notion that bad things create a fixed amount of blame which needs to be pinned on the people responsible – sometimes responsibility is 'shared', as though three people could each deserve one-third of the blame for something. If only blame were matched more tightly to the bad things people do, goes the myth, then people would not rob banks and not do any of the other bad things they do.

Now we see that the amount of responsibility is not fixed; it is not like property to be matched up with its owner. People can be responsible for bad things in degrees, depending on how much the likely consequences could influence their intentions. Several people might all be totally responsible for something, meaning the total amount of blame is much bigger than the total amount of bad things done. Alternatively, one person might be partly to blame, or no-one might be to blame at all, meaning some bad deeds should go unpunished. We shouldn't match blame to bad things in fixed proportions at all.

Newspaper editors, social commentators and cheap politicians should be reminded of this next time they suggest loose blame leads to a loose society. Then again, perhaps they are not free to suggest anything else, in which case they should be forgiven.

24 Punishment, Mercy and Remorse

'You have been found guilty of a wicked and selfish offence!' boomed the judge, staring down at the bank robber, now convicted and nervously awaiting his sentence. 'You have undermined the rules which are the foundation of a peaceful society, you put innocent staff and customers of the bank in great danger, and you were extremely reckless with a lethal firearm. In this courtroom, you have shown no sign of remorse. Before I issue a sentence for your crime, is there anything you would like to say – any that should be taken into consideration before your sentence is passed?'

The bank robber has, at least, a hope. 'A punishment wouldn't do any good', he pleads. 'I won't rob that bank again, whether I'm in prison or not, so what would locking me up actually achieve?'

To see this problem from a different angle, think back to the train crash dealt with by Sven in Chapter 5. Sven discovered a briefcase full of money that had been stolen from its owner. The thief admitted he stole it a few minutes before the disaster. This thief was a repeat offender who will never offend again because of his injuries from the train crash. Sven could see no benefit from punishing the thief, so he let him go. Instead, he decided 'do whatever's best' meant returning the briefcase to the dead passenger's family and pretending the theft never took place. This was a problem for the Enlightenment decision-making machine, 'do whatever has the best consequences', because it detached punishments from crimes. But why should they be linked together, and how? Why shouldn't the bank robber escape punishment too?

Almost all human societies have codes for punishment. Some are strict, others lenient. All establish some sort of link between the crime and the punishment, with the most severe penalties reserved for the most appalling crimes. Most westerns systems of law recognize four reasons for penalizing criminals. Punishment can protect the public; it can reform criminals so they don't offend again; it can deter them and others from committing further offences; and punishments provide retribution, a way for society to retaliate against a crime. Prisoners are usually locked up for at least two of these reasons, sometimes three or all four. Different reasons for punishment have been prominent at different times: protecting the public and deterring other crimes were most important a few centuries ago, while the emphasis on reforming prisoners has taken some time to develop. Politicians often debate which of these four reasons for punishment should influence judges most. Is there a 'right' way to determine the best link between crimes and punishments? Can we know exactly how strict or lenient we should be?

What is special about the thief on the train is that none of the first three reasons apply: the public doesn't need protecting because he's now crippled; the thief can't be reformed; and there is no deterrence factor. The only reason for punishing the thief on the train is retribution. Is retribution alone enough to justify punishment?

It turns out retribution and deterrence can't really be separated. Retribution is rather like paying an electrician for his work after he has done it. You promised to pay the electrician for his work beforehand, so it's right to pay him when he's finished. Similarly, we deter crime by promising to punish criminals which means we have to follow through. There *is* a reason to punish the criminal, even though sometimes it doesn't serve any direct purpose.

Chapter 16 showed whether an action was right should not depend directly upon when it takes place. Crimes should be punished *after* they happen as they would have been deterred *before* they happened. A punishment is a deterrent applied late. Some would say too late, but the punishment should still be applied – lateness does not make the punishment wrong. So the retribution for a crime should match the deterrent that would have been necessary to deter the crime before the crime was committed. Punishments should be measured so as to provide an effective deterrent, past or future, to the crime concerned.

We should *punish intentions that harmed others with the severity that would have been necessary to deter them before the crime* (unless mercy is due).

In other words, now we know how severely we should sentence the bank robber: we should sentence him with whatever sentence would have been necessary to deter him from robbing the bank before he did it. We *can* decide between those who call for lenient sentences and those who call for strict ones – we have an answer. Protecting the public, deterring others and reforming the criminal may influence how this sentence is applied. But, if the judge is working only on retribution, we can work out what the sentence should be.

But we still have another problem: mercy.

Empathy with a criminal, who may well offer an endearing reason why they did what they did, can be difficult to reconcile with maintaining effective punishments and deterrents. Empathy with a criminal would certainly make us think hard before we decided on a very severe punishment, or a punishment worse than the crime. Should we be merciful, or should we be strict?

We need a sincerity test, so criminals can't fake a false case for mercy. Courtrooms have come across this problem before and have already developed ways of deciding how much mercy an offender deserves. The best test is whether or not the criminal does something to rectify their crime. Criminals who compensate their victims have less of a crime to be punished for, and if they punish themselves through genuine remorse it means there is less cause for someone else to punish them. Also, criminals who manage to reform themselves very substantially can become a different person from the person who committed the crime, so again, it would be inappropriate to punish them as before. Finally, mercy should usually keep us from inflicting punishments worse than the original crimes. So, *mercy should reduce the punishment applied when the deterrent-based punishment would exceed the crime, when criminals punish themselves through sincere remorse, when they compensate their victims or when they change into a significantly different person.*

This line on mercy is important for us because it relates to the rather uncomfortable problem introduced in Chapter 20: aren't we responsible for all the deaths we could have prevented? Beyond the list of criminal actions there is a list of criminal *non*-actions in the world, and we would find that most of us are responsible for committing them. The disturbing fact is we are as responsible for deliberate non-actions as much as we are responsible for what we actually do. According to the system we have just outlined, this makes us suitable for punishment, and the punishment should be the minimum necessary to make us behave differently. What threat would you need to make you spend your lunch money on starving people elsewhere? That's not an easy question. Our best bet is to plea for mercy. And for this we should try to make amends, by trying to prevent future deaths. We will cover how we should do this in Chapter 36.

The bank robber's first act of remorse should be to give away his money, but he will still deserve a hefty sentence.

25 Something Funny about Promises

There's something funny about promises. We make promises but we also break them: two things which shouldn't go together. How can we both make promises, and break them? How can we keep doing it? There is something very funny about promises indeed.

Consider modern marriage. This is a public promise for life-long togetherness made by a couple and underwritten by their family, friends and, if they have one, their God. Yet society also sanctions divorce. How can that be? Whether you think divorce is acceptable or marriage is sacred, you have to agree the two positions are incompatible. Marriage is a promise about which society seems very confused.

Making a promise involves offering apparent certainty to someone; a promise is a commitment to act, which is different from the act itself. By making a promise at one time, you are committing yourself to take a certain course at a future time, even though new options may have emerged by then.

So, it seems there are three questions with promises:

1. When should you make a promise?
2. When should you break a promise you have already made?
3. And if a promise can be broken, is it still really a promise?

These questions have been discussed before, but most of the answers are incomplete. The Prussian philosopher Kant argued promises should be kept because he thought there was something nonsensical about deceitful promises. The British philosophers Jeremy Bentham and John Stuart Mill argued promises should usually be kept because breaking them would make people worse off, although they could be broken occasionally or secretly, as long as general trust in promises was not shaken. Scottish thinker William David Ross, writing at the time of the Great Depression, said promises must be kept as a matter of duty; they might need to be broken from time to time, but there couldn't be a formula to say when these times would be. These views are all interesting, but none of them really offers practical, everyday advice on which promises to make and which to break.

The full Help Principle is more useful. 'Help someone if the all-time direct value of your help is worth more to them than it is to you' indicates we need to compare two things when deciding whether or not to make a promise: the value to the person who receives it, and the value of keeping your options open. So, if a promise allows someone to plan in a certain way, and you were probably going to do something anyway, then you should make the promise. If you promise to have food ready for someone when they get home from work, the value of your promise is the extra work they can get done because they know they won't have to buy food on the way home, and the cost of the promise is not doing whatever else might arise because you're cooking. Only if the extra work is worth more than the 'whatever else' should you make the promise.

So the rule on making promises is: *make a promise only if it instils certainty worth more than the best option your promise rules out.*

What of the second problem – when should promises be broken? The answer is not 'never' – even sincere promises need to be broken from time to time. Politicians are often very sincere in their promises and they know the electorate will punish them if they break them, but even their sincere promises may have to be broken when a national emergency strikes.

We need to apply the Help Principle again, this time to a promise that has already been made. This involves comparing the value of promise with the value of the promise-breaking option. The Help Principle tells us we should break promises when something new and very important arises and the original promise doesn't have much value. Breaking the promise must be worth more to you than keeping your word is to the person who was promised.

Hence the rule on when to break a promise is: *keep your promises, unless they are worth less to others than a new option is to you.*

Note that this isn't a comparison between the two options. It's not saying 'would you prefer to do the thing you promised or something else?' – that would just amount to ignoring the promise completely. You have to compare the value of the promise with the *extra* value achieved by breaking the promise for the new option.

These two rules together reveal something else about promises. Because the motive for making a promise and the motive for keeping a promise are different, there are times when it will be appropriate to both make *and* break a promise. A promise to a kidnapper, for example, offering that, if he comes out with his hostage unharmed he won't be punished is just such a promise: there's a good reason to make the promise, and also a good reason to break it soon after. This also means occasionally, as with the promise to the kidnapper, there are reasons not to believe the promise will be kept. This possibility threatens the whole concept of promises – there are times when promises just don't mean anything anymore, such as between two warring factions who have lost all trust for each other.

What can be done to reinforce these most dubious promises? Someone could offer a 'promise to keep a promise', but this is paradoxical – if a second promise is needed to reinforce the first, then it just highlights the weakness of the first promise. A 'promise to keep a promise' is self-defeating promise; it undermines the credibility of the main promise it seeks to enhance. This is the 'paradox of promises'.

This takes us to the third problem. If a promise can be broken, is it still really a promise?

To resolve this we need a definition: a promise is 'sincere' if the promise-maker truly expects to fulfil it at the decisive moment. So, if at 9 a.m. I promise to meet you at 3 p.m., that promise is sincere if, in the morning, I really expect to be there on time. Something can happen at noon which means I break my word, but it was still a sincere promise as long as I didn't see it coming when I made the commitment to you.

It will only be right to break a sincere promise if there is change in circumstances in the time between the promise being made and the moment for decision. For this change to be enough to justify breaking the promise it must be more important than the breach of trust it could cause. So, something that justifies breaking a sincere promise must be relevant; it must be more important than the promise; it must be unforeseen when the promise was made; and, since the promise-maker should make a reasonable attempt to predict important things that may arise, the change should be unforeseeable with reasonable effort.

This gives us more detail on when to break a promise: *a sincere promise should only be broken if there's a relevant, unforeseen and reasonably unforeseeable change more important than the promise itself which arises between when the promise is made and the time to keep it.* Breaking a promise does not remove the original commitment. A broken promise is still a promise: we have answered the third of the three questions about promises.

Promise-breakers can indicate they didn't mean to break their promise by apologizing, offering compensation and applying the Help Principle. *If you break a promise, try to compensate the people whose trust you lose.* As with other intentions that go awry, people should show they're sorry.

People sometimes break promises but pretend they haven't. I could promise I had given up cigarettes then wander away for a subtle smoke. Even if you never found out I broke the promise to you, something would be wrong. Since breaking a promise doesn't alter the original-commitment it created, breaking a promise but pretending not to amounts to lying about the broken promise. In other words, it creates two problems: a lie, as well as the broken promise. These problems do not cancel each other out (although they may mean the promise-breaker escapes punishment). Both problems need to be dealt with. So: *breaking a promise in secret compounds the breach with a lie; it does not provide an excuse.*

There *is* something funny about promises. At least three things, in fact. But the Help Principle seems to be able to explain them all.

It took more than 2 years for the most famous lie in American political history to run its course. Between June 1972, when security guard Frank Wills became suspicious of a small piece of tape keeping open a basement door on a building in Washington DC, and August 1974, when President Nixon announced his resignation, 'Watergate' was a story with many different episodes, aspects and sub-plots. There was a torrent of detail about the break-in at the Democratic campaign headquarters and its repercussions, which showed the White House to be engaged in a confusing range of dubious activities. Amid all these accusations, the charge which was by far the most destructive was that the President lied to the American people: once proven, it forced him to resign. This was not the worst accusation, so why was it the most damaging?

There is no answer to be found in the rarity of lying: lies are common. When did you last tell a lie? If you claim it was more than a day ago you're probably lying now. Most people lie most days. Just count up how many times you distorted the truth during your most recent conversation. Most of us mislead others a lot. You're probably used to the amount you deceive others. We often lie with little thought. We have certain answers ready for certain questions and these answers are often quite untruthful – when people ask us how we are we usually give much less than a fully rounded account. Some social events would go seriously awry without these insincere pleasantries. Lying and deception are so deeply ingrained in the way we live our lives, it's hard to imagine life without them. Some people mislead so often it can be surprising other people ever believe them at all. Yet, at the same time, we don't like being lied to. Lies corrode the relationship between people. They make you feel distrusted, even dirty. Lying takes away a person's ability to control their own life because it forces them to act on distorted information.

Problems about lying vexed ancient writers, but they concern popular modern writers even more: newspapers are always hunting out lies and liars. Journalists scour the words of public figures looking for untruths and deceptions, even more so since Watergate. It's almost a game: everybody knows politicians lie – if you can catch one at it, the journalist wins and the politician loses. Lies are usually easier to explain than more complex misdemeanours, and so more destructive.

Liars like Nixon break an implicit promise to tell the truth. We make this promise to tell the truth just by speaking. This promise to tell the truth is not explicit. It cannot be: if we added 'and that's the truth' to everything we said it would hardly reinforce confidence in our words. Just like the paradox of promises explained earlier, we cannot make a form of communication stronger with the same form of communication. Hence, we have to assume most of us are telling the truth most of the time.

The assumption we're being told the truth is backed up by something we're all taught from an early age: lying is wrong. Lying is bad, and nobody ever says it's good. Deception is defended occasionally, when it's labelled 'discretion' or 'politeness', but lying is condemned almost without exception.

So: we condemn lying but we all still do it. This makes most parents hypocritical: they tell their offspring to be truthful while they lie themselves. The common prohibition against lying is a lie itself. This is spectacular proof that common moral views are inadequate. Just think of the newspapers which castigated Nixon for lying: most of them regularly distort the truth in their choice of the news agenda, yet they feel no remorse for this hypocrisy.

We clearly need a rule on lying. Not just the simple rule that 'lying is wrong', because we know that sometimes it's appropriate to lie. We need to know when lying is *really* wrong, and when it's right.

Aristotle didn't think such a rule was possible: anybody who advocated lying could never be believed, he said. Certainly, if there was a rule for lying, it is hard to see how people would believe anything when the rule applied. Also, there are lots of paradoxes which involve lying, such as someone who introduces themselves with 'the first thing I tell people when I meet them is a lie'. If what they say is true then it's a lie, and if it's a lie then it's true. If a general rule on lying could apply to itself, it could be nonsensical too.

We have a problem. The rule on lying taught to 5-year-olds, 'don't tell lies', is not credible because we all tell so many, but any other rule to justify lying looks like it could be self-defeating. Can there be a credible rule which tells us when to lie?

The answer is yes, there can be. To find it, we need to think again about when it's right to lie. The fact we all lie so often indicates there must be something good about them. Fiction is a whole industry based on lies, providing us with entertainment and pleasure. We volunteer to hear lies when we watch a movie or read a novel. Stories would be boring without them. But most lies are slightly different from fiction-as-entertainment because they don't have this voluntary element. A proper lie involves feeding someone a falsehood with an intent to mislead them when they had an appetite for the truth.

Lies have value because they can correct problems elsewhere: diplomats use lies to stop much greater evils, such as wars; road signs which threaten us with pretend punishments can make us drive more safely. Perhaps the best example of a 'good lie' is the placebo effect: giving sick patients a dummy pill and telling them they will recover really can improve their health. The placebo effect can help people overcome terrible diseases and injuries.

So lies can be good: they can alter people's behaviour in good ways. Someone whose health is restored through the placebo effect has clearly been helped by a lie – their renewed health is the value a lie can bring. If a lie prevents a war, then the value of the lie is the value of the peace. If a lie prevents a car crash, then the value of the lie is the value of avoiding the accident.

But lies carry a downside, too: when you lie you break the implicit promise to tell the truth. Lies are broken promises.

How bad is a lie? Lies erode trust – people will believe the liar much less in the future, and it is this loss of trust which determines how bad a lie is. Note that lies exposed and lies which remain undetected both involve the same broken promise, the same implicit promise to tell the truth – they are both equally bad. It doesn't matter that one is discovered while the other succeeds. So to gauge how bad is a lie which is not found out, the loss of trust has to be imagined. To calculate the cost of a lie, it is the cost of lost trust that would result *if the lie were discovered*.

So now we have the components we need to apply the Help Principle and work out when it's right to lie. Help comes in the form of changing someone's behaviour with a lie, but comes with a cost – the cost of lost trust that would result if the lie were discovered. Someone wondering what to tell the cancer patient has to decide whether the patient would like having her health boosted, even if she subsequently discovered it was on the basis of an untruth. The Help Principle suggests a lie should be told if it induces changes in behaviour worth more than the general loss of value in communications, past and future, to which the lie would lead *were it discovered* (whether the lie actually is exposed or not).

So the rule on lying is this: *Deceive only if you can change behaviour in a way worth more than the trust you would lose, were the deception discovered (whether the deception actually is exposed or not).*

Note that this rule also caters for general deception – the half-truths and misleading statements we often make which are not quite full lies. And since there is no moral difference between an action and a deliberate non-action that shares the same intended outcome, it follows there is no moral difference between a spoken lie and deliberately staying silent with the intention that someone will believe the falsehood. Deception, lies, staying silent when you know someone believes the wrong thing: it's all the same really.

There is a serious practical problem with the rule on lying which can make it hard to apply. You can never actually compare the positive impact of a lie with how much people actually detest being lied to. If the doctor asks the cancer patient, 'Do you want me to heal you with the placebo effect, or would you rather be told the truth?' the placebo will have been neutered. If you give people the option of being lied to, the option disappears. The only way to avoid this practical problem is for the liar to imagine themselves in the mind of the person they might lie to. They have to empathize. Good lies require imagination by the liar.

There is something else we can work out about when it is right to lie: lies can only be right when people don't behave normally. To see this, think about how we act and react to things. We are all naturally attuned to behaving most appropriately for the circumstances we perceive – so when it's cold, we soon learn to put on extra clothes. When we get something wrong we try to correct ourselves next time. Through trial and error, we learn to behave the right way for most situations.

If it's right to lie, then this 'trial and error' system must be failing somehow. If I lie to you about the temperature outside, then there must be some reason why you would behave inappropriately on hearing the truth – for example, because you're more worried about the cold than you should be.

So justifying a deliberate deception requires a special reason to believe the person hearing it will not act appropriately when told the truth. Spelling this out as a rule, we should: *Communicate so people can do what's best for the real circumstances.* A justified lie requires a reason to believe the hearer would not act appropriately if told the truth. Because normally we do act appropriately for the situations we face, this means there always has to be a special reason to lie.

This is a useful maxim for the modern media which, through pressures of time, money and low attention spans, is hardly ever able to provide the public with the full and comprehensive truth. It has to summarize. Media should summarize so viewers, listeners and readers can do what's best for the real circumstances.

Communicate so people can do what's best for the real circumstances is also a good maxim for politicians: if people would behave inappropriately when told the truth – for example, panic buying a vital commodity because they're told it's scarce – then a lie might be justified. But the maxim also provides no defence for Nixon: what he did was wrong, and he was wrong to lie about it. This is a credible rule on lying – it can even be adapted for 5-year-olds: 'only lie on special occasions', and we even have an answer ready in case they ask what a special occasion is: it's when the change in behaviour induced by the lie is worth more than cost of lost trust were the lie discovered.

Perhaps if we were more truthful when we told our children about lying, our defences against lies would be more robust. And if everybody could tell the difference between good lies and bad lies, politicians like Nixon who told very bad lies would be caught much sooner.

27 Rules for Romance and Sex

What does it mean to 'do whatever's best' in love? The Enlightenment decision-making machine takes us nowhere when it comes to romance.

Romance and sex are ignored by most theories on how the world should be. Even the religionists, old and new, who lay down strict codes of conduct for sex, do not back up their commands with any sort of analysis: romance and sex are merely attributed to the mysteries of God and the basis of His commands is left equally unclear. Meanwhile, the poets, lyricists and scriptwriters who *do* have something to say about romance or sex rarely offer systematic answers to the drier topics of moral theory – how much people should be punished, when countries should intervene in other countries, and so on. Yet romance and sex are central to many people's lives. They are discussed more than promises and lies, and probably more than money and morals. We are missing out on very common concerns if we ignore them.

There have been a few efforts. Kant was disgusted by the idea of people 'using' each other for sex and regarding it as a 'degradation of human nature'. He thought good moral relations ruled out sexual relations, unless people agreed to a life-long marriage contract – a view that seems dated to many people nowadays. Hobbes, by contrast, advocated lust on the basis that it mixed a desire to please with a desire to be pleased, so sex was just a way of being good to each other. Hobbes' view, for different reasons than Kant's, also seems to miss something important. Neither thinker provided comprehensive and credible advice on this topic.

This makes romance and sex an interesting test for the Help Principle. If we can apply our rules to romance and sex as well as everything else then we have something very special indeed.

Romance first – can we apply the Principles to romance? And if we do, what does the theory tell us to do?

Most societies which allow people to choose their own partners have complex etiquettes which govern the choosing process. People invite each other to dances, or respond to advances in certain ways, or send anonymous valentine cards. Pairs of people sometimes feel a spontaneous mutual attraction; more often, they are unsure about how to proceed with potential partners. Most etiquettes which govern the pairing process have a certain scope for ambiguity to allow for this. One or both partners is expected to give signals with more than one meaning – does she fancy me, or is she just being friendly? Relationships deepen, linger in some intermediate state or conclude as a no-hoper. Relationships can move from one category to another – a no-hope relationship can suddenly become a promising prospect; or a deep relationship can cool into a lingering uncertainty. Relationships fall into one or other category or change between them on the basis of the feelings of each partner, and according to signals each receives from the other.

That's a very concise account of the current system. Usually it is more complex, and obviously, the system varies from person to person and place to place. A half-smile is interpreted as a sullen rejection in some cultures; in others, it is a flirtatious invitation. Also, the system changes according to age: appropriate behaviour for a 16-year-old might not be acceptable for a 30-something. Some people want brief liaisons, others want something longer lasting, and there are various codes to cope with this. The fact there is this wide variation between different groups of people doing essentially the same sort of thing is interesting in itself. We will examine these differences later.

Despite all these complexities, romance is essentially about three simple things: feelings, communication and making promises. Since we have already managed to extend the Help Principle into these areas and developed rules for them, we should be able to work out some universal rules for romance by applying the Help Principle to love.

Romantic relationships are all about person-to-person wants. If you love someone, you want to see them prosper – this is the bonus benefit that comes from enjoying other people do well, explained in Chapter 18. We should apply the Help Principle to our potential partners as we should apply it to others but, if we love our partner, then there will be more bonus benefits. It is these bonus benefits which matter with romance. In other words, ideal relationships will provide both parties with maximum bonus benefits; each should enjoy seeing the other person prosper as much as possible.

Bonus benefits increase when people are well-paired. If the people inside the pairings choose their partners for themselves, they must be good at assessing potential partners for suitability. This, in turn, requires people to understand their own emotions and those of their potential partners, all in reasonable time. The better people are at empathizing with other people, the better they will be at choosing partners.

A central part of this process involves people signalling their emotions to potential partners. Some people are deceptive here – they give misleading messages to keep the other person interested, or to pretend they are not interested when in fact they are. Part of this is simply ambiguity: people are not sure of their own feelings, so they are not sure what feelings to display to others. But the deception can also be more deliberate. People might enjoy being pursued by others, or they may feel embarrassed about their affection for the other person.

Using the rule on lying, we can establish when this deception will be justified. Lying is only justified when the change in behaviour it induces is worth more than the cost of lost trust, were the deception discovered. So, flirting with someone you don't like can only be justified if it actually inspires a relationship, that is, it changes your *own* feelings, as well as the other person's. This could be expressed as a rule: don't flirt with someone unless you might mean it. Deception the other way – when you pretend not to like someone but really you do – can again only be justified if it makes a good relationship more likely. So, people should only pretend – falsely – they don't like someone if they think it will make the relationship more likely, for example, by providing more time for friendship to develop. Putting these two together, it seems we should only misrepresent our feelings if we hope to change them, or foster a relationship.

There is a problem with this because it can lead to a sort of paradox. An amorous pursuer will mistake rejection for exactly this sort of deception. 'He's only saying "no" to spur me on!' she might say. This will extend the pursuit, and lead to dissatisfaction all round. The way to resolve this paradox is for two different sorts of rejection. There needs to be a flirtatious 'probably not', which really means 'probably yes', and a clear 'no', which means exactly that. Someone who continues the pursuit despite a clear 'no' is misguided and should desist.

So, by applying the Help Principle and the rule on lying, we can set out some fairly clear basic rules for the earlier stages of romance. There will be more, but these are the first:

1. try to assess your own feelings towards someone else in reasonable time;
2. empathize with others to assess your mutual suitability;
3. don't flirt with someone unless you might mean it, and reject unwanted advances politely but clearly;
4. do not pursue people you are not interested in, or who are clearly not interested in you;
5. underrepresent your affection to someone only if you think doing so will foster the relationship; and
6. in general, express your affection, uncertainty or disinterest clearly, unless there is a special reason not to.

These rules represent a marked improvement on the old maxim of 'all's fair in love (and war)'. They are practical and fairly simple, and they can apply to a wide spectrum of different practices in different cultures. They require an awareness of oneself and the impact of one's behaviour on others: they are rooted in empathy, which is a good place for love to be based. They also offer a remedy to much romantic disappointment: most heartache comes when assumptions about another person shatter; those assumptions often arise from an act of affection that person has made. If people connect their inner feelings with their outward displays of affection more clearly, heartbreak would be rarer and less painful.

We are now able to provide an answer to Sue, whose problem was set out in Chapter 2 of this book. Sue had agreed to go to a dance with John. John bought both of them tickets and looked forward to the event. Later, Sue was invited by Steve, with whom she would much rather go. Sue wanted to know what she should do: take up Steve's offer and upset John? Or keep her promise to John, and miss out on going with Steve? She also wanted to know whether she should lie to either of them.

She has already made a commitment to go to the dance with John. We will not examine whether she was right to make that commitment (that depends on how foreseeable it was that Steve would ask her to the dance), but we do need to know exactly what sort of commitment it was. She could have agreed to go to the dance with John in several ways. It could have been a strictly limited acceptance that John would buy her ticket, or it could have been loaded with much more romantic significance. John may have misinterpreted what Sue agreed to – another complicating factor if he did – but assuming he did not, Sue seems to have agreed to something a little more than just an offer of a ticket, but not much more.

When Steve invited Sue to the dance, she was given a motive to break her promise to John. Should she? The Help Principle says she should compare the value of her promise to John with the extra attractions of going to the dance with Steve rather than John. This comparison requires other answers – how much does she prefer Steve to John? Is the dance a unique occasion or will there be other chances to meet Steve? How hurt will John be if she doesn't go with him? These questions show Sue's situation is more intricate than it might appear. But they also show that, by applying the Help Principle and the rule on promise breaking, it *is* possible for Sue to work out what she should do. Basically, if she prefers Steve by a great amount, or if she made only a small commitment initially, then she should go with Steve. Alternatively, if she prefers Steve by only a little, if there will be other opportunities to meet him and if she made a substantial commitment to John, then she should stick with her initial decision. It may take Sue some skill to decide which of these scenarios she is in, but the Help Principle has successfully answered the 'right or wrong' part of her problem.

There was an extra problem for Sue: should she lie to either of them, whatever she does? Again, now we have an answer for this. She should deceive only if the person she is deceiving won't respond appropriately when told the truth. So, how will John react if she tells him she's going with Steve? Sue needs to establish this fact to find out whether or not she should lie, but the point is now what she should do just that: a matter of fact. She only needs to understand her situation to know what to do. The 'right' and 'wrong' part of it has been resolved.

Empathy, obligation and the Help Principle can be applied to sex, too. The Autonomy Principle, for example, suggests people choosing their own sexual partners will be a lot better than people having their partners chosen for them. This extends to the sort of partners they choose: unless you know someone's sexuality better than they can (which will be very difficult), there is no direct reason to interfere with them being homosexual, heterosexual or having multiple partners. Guidance is only appropriate when someone is unable to cope with the power or consequences of sex, and is unable to adjust their own behaviour to accommodate this fact. Hence, sex education should make people aware of the impact and dangers of sex, but not impose sexual preferences on them.

The Help Principle can also arbitrate between Hobbes' and Kant's different views on sex. If sex counts as just another form of help, then the Help Principle could be changed into the rule: 'have sex with someone if it is worth more to them than it is to you'. By this rule, everybody who wanted sex a lot should be granted it by most other people. Sex would become as common and as insignificant as any other form of human interaction (to his credit, not even Hobbes went this far). But this rule misapplies the Help Principle because it ignores the rule on direct help which owes much to Kant: we should always treat people according to their own wants and intentions, not what others want of them. It doesn't matter how much someone wants sex with someone else, people should have sex only with people they want to have sex with – *both* parties must be enthusiastic. This then creates a responsibility on each partner to ensure the other is fully aware of the wider consequences of the act; sex procured through lies or a disregard for the other person's feelings is no good. Sex becomes an act of mutual respect. This is closer to Hobbes' positive view of sex than Kant's prudish disgust of it, although the logic behind it owes more to Kant than to Hobbes. The Help Principle takes the best of both views and leads to a distinctly twenty-first-century approach to sex: *have sex only with people you want to have sex with, be aware of the potential impact, and ensure it is an act of mutual respect.*

The list of rules on romance and sex in this chapter is far from complete – the rules could be extended to cover reproductive sex, safe sex, and so on, but that is for elsewhere. But they do demonstrate that the principles in this book can be applied to areas not normally suited to this sort of analysis. It is further confirmation that the Help Principle is *the* central basis for how people should interact.

28 How to Choose in Small Groups

How should groups make decisions?

If you are a democrat you may have an answer already: just put it to a vote. But this answers a slightly different question. Democracy offers a method for putting together lots of individual decisions *once they are already made*, usually based on the idea of every person getting an equal say. We need to know *how* people should cast their vote. What should influence them? Democracy's fine, but it doesn't work if people vote on the basis of hairstyles, sound bites or racist prejudices. Nonsense in, nonsense out. Democracy often runs into problems even if people vote just on their own personal interest, because what's best for the group isn't always what's best for the majority. So, how *should* people vote? What should people look for when they make group decisions?

This question is not answered by many of the world's democratic constitutions: most of these great texts set out the rules of the game but don't tell people how to play it. Voters are left to decide for themselves how they should make up their minds. Political parties offer conflicting advice, adding to the confusion. The old communist 'Peoples' Democracies' of eastern Europe used to advise people much more: they should vote for the best communist, if they were allowed to vote at all. But the case for communism was never convincing, and most of these countries have now abandoned it. Some religion-based states make group decisions based on holy texts – principally the Bible and the Quran. But, as we saw in Chapter 3, unless these theocracies can demonstrate why one religion is better than another, there is no reason to believe any of them.

The American writer John Rawls came up with one of the most impressive answers to 'how should groups make decisions?' in 1971. Once people had as many universal liberties as possible, said Rawls, groups should make decisions so the worst-off person benefits as much as possible – his so-called 'Difference Principle'. Making the worst-off person as well-off as possible has an intuitive egalitarian appeal, and Rawls could put forward a compelling explanation for it. His approach offers clearer advice than the constitutions of most democracies, without resorting to superstition like most theocracies.

Unfortunately, as we saw in Chapter 13, Rawls' work has at least one key flaw: although he showed a clear basis for his thinking, he could only arrive at his 'Difference Principle' by deliberately setting out for it. He came up with something intuitively appealing because he started with his intuitions in the first place. We need an answer that does not rely on intuitions or at least gives us an independent reason why our intuitions may be right.

What we are looking for is a formula for making the right decisions in groups. Alas, the Help Principle isn't yet up to the task – it is just for two people. It's one-to-one. That's fine as long as there are just two people, but clearly the world is more crowded than that. We need to extend the Help Principle so it can apply in groups.

For the answer, we need to return briefly to the roots of the Help Principle – to empathy and obligation. Like the Help Principle, empathy and obligation also only apply between individuals. When we empathize, we imagine the concerns of another individual as if they were our own; we cannot do this with groups of individuals other than to treat each member separately. Even when you empathize with a defeated sports team, for example, you empathize with individuals who are members of that team. You do not imagine how bad it is to be the whole team; you imagine yourself as a member of that losing team. With obligations too, our duties towards a group derive from our moral obligations towards each group member – our obligations to society depend entirely on our obligations to each person it contains. So helping a group should involve treating each member of the group individually and acting on each one's concerns. But what does this actually mean in practice?

This point is best explained through an example. Imagine three people in a car deciding which way to turn at a junction. Two people want to drive down the hill to a cinema because there is a film they both want to see; the third is an out-patient who wants to drive up the hill for an appointment with his doctor. The appointment and the start of the film are both quite soon: the car can drive to one or the other, but there is not time to do both. Crucially, the third person wants to go to the doctor much more than both the others who prefer the cinema. Should the car drive down to the film or up to the doctor? If the people in the car decide to vote on it and they cast their vote solely on the basis of what they want for themselves, they will drive down to the cinema (two votes) rather than up to the doctor (just one vote). Voting in this way ignores the fact that the out-patient wants to keep their appointment with the doctor much more than the others want to see the film.

Instead of voting, the passengers could apply the Help Principle to each other. Each of the three passengers applies the Help Principle to each other as a one-to-one relationship, so the Principle is applied three times.

When the Help Principle is applied between the two who want to see the film it doesn't make any difference to them. Neither has something worth giving to the other, so it doesn't affect their choices. But when these two apply the Help Principle to the third, they will both give way. For both of them, their help, in the form of allowing the car to drive up to the doctor rather than down, is worth more to that third person than it is to them. So, when the passengers apply the Help Principle to each other, the group will choose the alternative favoured by the minority: they will drive up to the doctor, even though more people prefer to drive the other way.

You can repeat examples like this one with various differences – more options, more people, different preferences, and so on. From all these examples, there is a general pattern which emerges: if every member of a group applies the Help Principle to every other member, the person who can benefit most from any decision should always take priority. The number of individuals benefiting from that option doesn't matter. What matters is who needs something most. So the rule for making decisions in small groups is this: *Choose whichever option benefits any individual the most.*

'Choose whichever option benefits any individual the most' may seem like an odd rule. It means the number of people who benefit from an option has no bearing on whether that option is the right one. All that matters is *how much* they benefit. Democrats should raise an eyebrow at this.

But John Rawls, if he were still alive, probably would not. Although the rule for making decisions in small groups is not in line with his Difference Principle, it does cohere with his first principle, that people should have maximum personal liberty as long as other people also have those liberties. This is because personal liberties are most important to the person they affect. When regimes lock away their dissidents, it causes greater harm to the dissidents than any benefit it brings to any other person. Just as Rawls' first principle would outlaw arbitrary imprisonment, so would the Help Principle's rule for decision-making in small groups.

So, next time you are asked to cast your vote in a small group, this is how to do it. Don't vote according to hairstyles, sound bites, racist prejudices or religion, *vote for whichever option benefits any individual the most.*

29   How to Choose in Large Groups

'Choose whichever option benefits any individual the most' may seem fine in small groups, but is it appropriate in larger ones? Can massive national democracies really be run on this principle?

Suppose a million people in a country are happy with their national flag, but one citizen passionately wants to change it to his favourite colour, turquoise. If we apply the rule 'choose whichever option benefits any individual the most', this turquoise fetishist will win through. A million people will have to change their flag just to satisfy one person obsessed with a certain colour. If there were only three people in the country, two of whom didn't care very much, deciding on a turquoise flag to suit the third might be reasonable, but not if there are a million. It matters whether the flag serves three people or a million. Our rule to 'choose whichever option benefits any individual the most' seems more plausible in small groups than larger ones.

The idea of a flag serving its people is novel: most countries expect their people to serve the flag. US President John F Kennedy famously implored his fellow Americans to 'ask not what your country can do for you – ask what you can do for your country.' It is a demand made many times throughout history by almost every country with an army, and many people have obeyed it – in extreme cases sacrificing their lives in service of the state.

This is where the problem arises: self-sacrifice for the group does not fit at all with 'choose whichever option benefits any individual the most'. The two concepts are at opposite ends of a very long spectrum. At one extreme, we can prioritize the individual with our rule for decision-making in small groups, but this seems to exclude the possibility that it can ever be right for someone to give their life in the group interest. At the other extreme, we have Sven and his brutal interior police force, with all the inhumanities set out in Chapter 5 that can arise if everything – including people – become subservient to the group interest or state. We need to be able to reconcile these extreme positions, so both individuals and groups can make the right decisions. And it's not enough to say the solution lies somewhere between the two extremes: that's just intuition. To reconcile the two, we need to say exactly where the compromise should be.

To unlock this problem, reconsider the rule for deciding in small groups; 'choose whichever option benefits any individual the most'. The rule emerges because the Help Principle applied between two people favours whichever individual benefits most, so when everybody in a group applies the Principle, the group should also choose in favour of whichever individual has most at stake. This assumes everyone reciprocates or shows gratitude for all help they are offered, enabling the Help Principle to be applied in full. When people do not reciprocate the help they are offered – either because they are selfish or because the group is too large for them to return help to every person – the reciprocity rule affects the way the Help Principle operates. Decision-making in groups *without* reciprocity is different from decision-making *with* reciprocity, and this means it requires a different rule for how to make decisions.

To see how large groups should make decisions, imagine that instead of a car, there is now a big bus full of people deciding which way to turn at the junction. Still only one person on the bus has an important doctor's appointment and wants to go uphill to the surgery, but now thirty others want to drive the bus downhill to watch the film. The bus is too big for the out-patient to thank all the other passengers for the sacrifice he is asking them to make. He can try to say 'thank you' to the people near him at the front, but he can't reach the people at the back of the bus before he has to get off. This means the passengers at the back are being asked to give help without the prospect of receiving any sort of help or gratitude in return. When these passengers apply the reciprocity rule, 'apply the Help Principle to others as much as they apply it themselves', they no longer need to give way to the out-patient: the out-patient will not apply the Help Principle to them, so they have no obligation to apply it to him. While the out-patient and those he would thank want to drive up to the doctor, the passengers at the back will want the option that benefits them – the cinema.

Just as when there were only three people in the vehicle, a choice must be made between benefits to the out-patient, and the more substantial, but dissipated, total benefits to the others. Now, though, because the out-patient will not reciprocate help to his fellow passengers, the dissipated total benefits to the other passengers can be expressed as reciprocity one person owes but does not deliver – that is, as benefits for one person. This is important because it means we can compare the benefits to the out-patient with the total compensation he owes to the passengers at the back. If the total benefits to several passengers of going downhill are greater than they are to the out-patient, then the bus should drive down to the cinema. *When there is no reciprocity, as in very large groups, we should go for whichever option brings the greatest total benefits, not the one which benefits any individual the most.*

So, if the doctor's appointment is potentially life-saving, driving the bus uphill is still the right thing to do. But if the appointment is more trivial, if there are lots of passengers at the back whom the out-patient never thanks or compensates, or if the film is important in some way, then it may be best to drive down to watch the film. Although in small groups we should choose whichever option benefits an individual the most, this no longer applies when thousands or millions of people stand to lose out. When really large numbers of people are involved, reciprocity is impossible so we should make decisions by adding the total benefits and total losses to everybody.

Making decisions in large groups, where there is no reciprocity, means choosing whichever option brings about the greatest total benefits. We know from previous chapters we should not just seek any benefits – it's all-time direct benefits that matter. So, the rule for making decisions in large groups is: *choose whichever option brings about the greatest total all-time direct benefits.*

This rule incorporates President Kennedy's dictum: it encourages people to make certain sacrifices for the common good. Indeed, there is a danger it goes too far. Everything could be subsumed in favour of the 'greatest all-time direct benefits'. Just like Sven's crazed existence in the brutal secret police, this new rule seems to make the group too important and the individual insignificant.

Although the rules for large groups and smaller groups clash, they don't contradict each other because they cover different cases. One deals with situations where there is reciprocity, and the other covers deals where there is none. When the beneficiary reciprocates all the help they receive (generally small groups) we should: 'choose whichever option helps any individual the most'. When the beneficiary does *not* reciprocate the help they receive (generally larger groups) we should: 'choose whichever option brings about the greatest total benefit'. Which rule applies depends upon how much the beneficiary reciprocates, or is grateful for, sacrifices made on his behalf.

Which rule should we use? Sometimes the line between the two situations is not so clear. The individual who stands to benefit a great deal might reciprocate help to most of the group, but not quite everyone. There could be fewer people in the bus – just how many do there have to be before we switch rules? Fifteen passengers? Twelve? There will always be borderline cases, and these make it difficult to know which rule to apply. We need a single rule which somehow combined both the others, so there was no need to make this sometimes difficult decision.

Fortunately, there is a way to do this. In a small group, when the individual reciprocates all the help they receive, it means the others do not really lose out. They might miss their film, but the gratitude shown by the person whom they help should make up for this. When the all-time benefits are considered – the benefits in the future, as well as the benefits now – it seems the decision to drive up to the doctor actually maximizes all-time benefit. When the future value of reciprocity is added in, the rule for small groups, 'choose whichever option benefits any individual the most' transforms into the rule for large groups, 'maximize all-time direct benefit'. Thinking in terms of all-time benefits reconciles the rules for making decisions with and without reciprocity. 'Choose whichever option brings about the greatest all-time direct benefit' actually caters for both small and large groups.

Alas, the all-time direct benefit is just too abstract to measure in most real-life situations. It means the future benefit for everybody, plus the past benefit (gains made in the past because of the decision taken since), all adjusted according to how much each person owes or is owed from the past. This can be very hard to contemplate, let alone to gauge.

Nevertheless, it is the right thing to gauge. Including the past benefits of a decision enables justice to be brought into social decision-making. It means the concerns of someone who helps others outweigh the concerns of someone who doesn't care. If the person wanting to take the bus to the doctor had a saintly record of helping others in the past, this should count in their favour when deciding whether to drive uphill or down. If they had never helped others, then there is much less reason to help them now.

This can be applied on a larger scale, too. If the people to benefit from a large project are more likely to reciprocate help than those who would lose out by the scheme, then this should affect whether or not the project goes ahead. A pious group with a history of helping others deserves to be favoured in social decision-making over less generous people. The many governments worldwide who rely on traditional 'cost–benefit analysis' (deciding on a large project if the total benefits exceed the total costs) need to adjust their thinking. However, it's rare for people on one side of a big social decision to be more generous than those on the other. The readiness to reciprocate help tends to be distributed evenly between different types of people. Unless there is clear evidence that the people on one side of a social dispute are more helpful than the others, it will usually be right to judge larger scale social projects by simply adding up the benefits of each option. There may be exceptions: war veterans, for example, have a proven record of helping others in the past which can merit special consideration in the future. But unless a group of people can demonstrate they have done more than what the average person *would* do, no special treatment is due.

So, it might just be possible someone who liked turquoise could have the flag changed as they wanted. If the turquoise fetishist had done something heroic or valuable to all the other million people, then a new national flag could be his reward. It would be an odd sort of reward, but then it would require a very odd sort of heroism.

Now we can reconcile the two extremes, placing ourselves on the scale between the individual on the one hand and the group on the other. Once reciprocity is factored in, and future and past benefits are counted up, there actually is only one place on the spectrum anyway – the spectrum disappears. We manage to avoid the inhumanities of Sven's brutal regime, while also allowing certain individual sacrifices to the group interest. We have a set of rules to govern small groups and massive national democracies alike.

Our system for making decisions is here, complete with proof and explanation. It can provide clear advice for many difficult issues, personal and public, small and big – from lying, to decision-making in groups, to allocating blame, and many others. It can correct our bad intuitions and confirm our good ones. It can even provide clear advice to Sven and Sue, who have needed advice since Chapter 2 – although not yet for us and how we should cope with the thousands of people dying daily from diarrhoea. We will come to that soon.

We also have three answers to the three basic questions of right and wrong: 'what characteristics should I have?', 'which outcome should I choose?' and 'what should I do?' These three ways of looking at right and wrong – ethics based on character, consequences and actions – do not have to be at odds. Since they all grow from the same DNA of right and wrong, they should all motivate people the same way. They turn out not to be alternatives, but different ways of explaining the same thing. Here is the advice offered by each of the three in turn:

What characteristics should I have?

The essence of being a good person involves treating the interests of other people as if they were your own. You can do this by imagining yourself in their situation (empathy) or imagining you have a special contract-like duty with them (obligation). You should empathize with others as they empathize; you have duties to others as far as they intend to act on duties themselves. It doesn't matter which way you do it – both ways amount to the same thing. Empathy and obligation are the most fundamental virtues.

This advice is useful, but it is not specific enough to address some important problems people face. It does not give detailed answers to any of the three quandaries set out in Chapter 2: Should Sven take the job with the brutal police force? Should Sue go to the dance with John or Steve? How should we deal with famine in Africa? Although empathy and obligation are worthy sentiments, we need more detail to make more complicated decisions.

Which outcome should I choose?

The twin virtues of empathy and obligation lead to the basic Help Principle – 'Help someone if your help is worth more to them than it is to you'. When this basic Help Principle is examined in depth it turns out to be shorthand for a fuller version – 'Help someone if the all-time direct value of your help is worth more to them than it is to you'. This fuller version is the right one.

This full Help Principle can be applied universally – if used correctly, it can answer any question of right and wrong. The difficulty is in applying it.

For example, consider whether to build a bridge to an isolated island. Choosing the right thing to do involves deciding whether to build or not to build. These are the steps in the decision-making process:

1. *Identify the options, noting that deliberately doing nothing is as much of an option as deliberately doing something.* Building the bridge will cost money which could be used elsewhere. So the options are: spend the money on the bridge, or spend it on something else.

2. *Find out who will be affected by each option and by how much.* The island dwellers are best able to say how valuable the bridge will be: they need to be asked whether they want it. Rival bids for the funds also need to be considered, and whoever will be providing the money should also be consulted.

3. *Include effects which have already happened.* If the bridge has already been promised, then someone might build a roadside café where the bridge would make landfall. If the bridge is then abandoned and their investment is lost, then this counts as a cost of not going ahead.

4. *Filter out person-to-person wants.* We shouldn't be guided by someone who enjoys seeing people suffer, so we shouldn't be influenced by people on other islands who may be jealous. The decision needs to be made according to how much each person benefits from the bridge or loses out because of it. When person-to-person wants are filtered out, you should have the all-time direct value of each option for each person.

5. *Apply the reciprocity rule to each person.* Someone who has helped others in the past or will help others more in the future counts for more than someone who is selfish. If the island dwellers have a record as being nicer than others, then this strengthens their case for the bridge to be built.

6. *Add it all up, and choose the best option.* The option which maximizes all-time direct benefit is best, so do it.

This approach differs markedly from simply 'choose whichever option has the best consequences' and old-style cost–benefit analysis. It involves adjusting for past-effects as well as consequences in the future; it involves filtering out person-to-person wants; it invites the recipients of help to take a role in deciding what's best for them; and it incorporates justice, by favouring good people over bad. Note also that, since it's intentions that count, what matters is trying to do the right thing.

Someone who tries to act on this advice but fails may be guilty of another fault, but they are better than someone who ends up following this advice by accident.

Still, this six-stage approach is not perfect. Although it leads to the rule for making decisions in small groups ('choose whichever option benefits any individual the most'), this is not immediately clear. The same is true of all the other rules which deal with promises, lies, and so on: this method will produce them, but it does not have them readily to hand. It is raw DNA: it contains the genetic code for all the decisions we need to make, but it does not breathe them into life. This approach will advise Sven to take up the job with the brutal interior police, but it will miss out on some of subtleties of the situation – it does not highlight the imperative to change the regime, for example, or say whether he should feel remorse for what he does. Also, this six-stage approach is cumbersome. If masses of people are involved, these calculations may be very difficult.

Also, this six-stage approach has a somewhat naïve view of decision-making. Life is not like choosing from menus – it's not about identifying options and choosing between them. Sometimes new options have to be created or imagined, and decisions come in chains and clusters; they are rarely isolated and discrete. You make one choice, this leads to a group of others, and then another group. Sometimes you need to treat these decisions separately, sometimes together – it's just the way life is. The six-stage process is ill-suited to this fact.

A final problem with this approach is that it threatens to detach people from the decision-making process. It's people that count; looking only at their direct gains and loses can be dangerously distracting. Like the reciprocity rule, this six-stage approach has a lethal edge. Thinking and acting well involves thinking about others as ourselves: we have to empathize to be good, and we should only abstract away from this if it clarifies what putting people first involves in complicated cases. Thinking in terms of 'all-time direct benefits' can be an abstraction too far.

For these reasons, rather than this one-method-fits-all approach, it's sometimes best to apply a set of principles and see which is most appropriate.

What should I do?

A more traditional definition of right and wrong involves labelling acts. Some are labelled 'right' and 'good', others are labelled 'wrong' and 'bad'. With a list of such acts, properly labelled, a person can decide which list an act belongs to, and so decide whether or not to do it.

We already have a list of principles for right and wrong, starting with the nine basic Principles set out in Chapter 22. To these, we can now add other principles dealing with punishment, promises, lying, and making decisions in small and large groups. Each of these themes will be summarized as a single principle for the sake of brevity, otherwise there will be simply too many principles. (The rules on romance and sex don't really belong here – they were an *application* of the rules on promises and lies applied to a specific area. If we included them then we ought to apply the Principles to a wide range of other areas and include those too.)

Chapters 23 and 24 looked at blame and punishment. We concluded several things, including:

- we should judge people by what they intend to make happen;
- luck shouldn't influence how people are judged;
- people are responsible for their actions as far as likely consequences could influence their intentions;
- there is no significant difference between an action and a deliberate non-action which share the same intended consequences;
- we should punish intentions that harmed others with the severity that would have been necessary to deter them before the crime, unless mercy is due; and
- mercy is due when the normal punishment would exceed the crime, when a person compensates their victim, when they punish

themselves through sincere remorse or when they become truly different from the person who committed the crime.

Summarizing all this into a single, lucid, memorable principle is not easy, but the essence is this, and it becomes the tenth principle:

10. *Ensure people who deliberately make bad things happen are punished as they should have been deterred, unless mercy is due.*

On promises, we have a similar array of conclusions from Chapter 25. We know:

- we should make a promise only if it instils certainty worth more than the best option the promise rules out;
- you should keep your promises unless they are worth less to others than a new option is to you;
- a sincere promise should only be broken if there's a relevant, unforeseen, and reasonably unforeseeable change more important than the promise itself which arises between when the promise is made and the time to keep it;
- breaking promises in secret compounds the breach with a lie; it does not provide an excuse; and
- if you break a promise, you should try to compensate the people whose trust you lose.

As with punishment, these are hard to summarize into a single conclusion. But, since the central problem with promises is knowing when to break them, the most useful principle is probably this:

11. *Keep your promises unless changing to a new option is worth more than the trust and plans you waste.*

Lying is equally complicated. In Chapter 26, we deduced:

- we should communicate so people can do what's best for the real circumstances;
- a justified lie requires a reason to believe the hearer would not act appropriately if told the truth;

- you should deceive only if you can change behaviour in a way worth more than the trust you would lose, were the deception discovered (whether the deception actually is discovered or not);
- lies should only be told on special occasions; and
- deliberately allowing someone to believe a falsehood amounts to a spoken lie.

From these, the basic principle on lying is this:

12. *Communicate so people can do what's best for the real circumstances.*

To these principles, we can add the two much easier principles for making decisions in small and large groups, from Chapters 28 and 29:

13. *In small groups, choose whichever option benefits any individual the most.*

And in large groups, when there is no reciprocity, the rule is:

14. *In large groups, choose whichever option has the best all-time outcome, by adding up the direct benefits and losses to people of each option.*

So, our full list of instructions is this:

1. *Seek value.*
2. *Empathize, and be true to your obligations.*
3. *Help someone if your help is worth more to them than it is to you.*
4. *Treat people according to their own wants and intentions, not by what others want of them.*
5. *Let people choose for themselves, unless you know their interests better than they can.*
6. *Apply the Help Principle to others as much as they would apply it themselves.*
7. *Defend someone who was attacked without due reason as if you were attacked yourself.*

8. *Try to enjoy providing and receiving help in line with the Help Principle.*

9. *Help others with humility, and express gratitude for help you receive.*

10. *Ensure people who deliberately make bad things happen are punished as they should have been deterred, unless mercy is due.*

11. *Keep your promises unless changing to a new option is worth more than the trust and plans you waste.*

12. *Communicate so people can do what's best for the real circumstances.*

13. *In small groups, choose whichever option benefits any individual the most.*

14. *In large groups, choose whichever option has the best all-time outcome, by adding up the benefits and losses to people of each option.*

These are the Principles of right and wrong. These define right and wrong; these are what people should do.

We could add to the list by dividing some of them into two principles, or by being more specific in certain areas. We could cover specific topics, such as the guidance 'have sex only with people you want to have sex with, be aware of the potential impact and ensure it is an act of mutual respect'. But greater detail also means greater distraction. Rather than listing more and more rules, it is better for people to think through problems and work out the relevant aspects for themselves. Detail is available if people need it, but people should deduce what these are when possible, and only be given them when necessary.

We need to pause. If any two of these Principles offered conflicting advice then people wouldn't be able to follow them both at the same time. The Principles wouldn't be able to motivate, and they would be flawed. And some of these Principles do come *close* to contradicting each other. For example, should you help a desperate gunman? Your help may be worth much more to him than it is to you, so the Help Principle would say 'yes'; but to protect people he may harm the duty to intervene could say 'no'. Apparent contradictions like this can be resolved, but the Principles need to be applied thoughtfully, and you need to be sure of the situation – is the gunman more dangerous or desperate?

Applied correctly, the Principles should never contradict each other because they all come from the same roots: empathy and obligation, through the Help Principle. They all derive from respecting value in others as well as oneself. It is this sentiment that needs to be applied; acting on these rules is only applying this sentiment indirectly. When the Principles appear to clash, it is because we are not applying them properly, and it's better to apply empathy and obligation directly. We empathize with the gunman, we remember our obligations to the people he may harm and we make a choice.

We have come full circle. When the virtues of empathy and obligation were too vague to tell us what to do, we used the six-stage process to get a detailed answer. When this became too mechanistic, we deferred to the 14 Principles for a more human approach. When these threatened to confuse, we went back to the twin virtues of empathy and obligation. There are advantages and disadvantages to all three approaches; different circumstances lend themselves to each one. But all three have evolved from the same stuff, the same DNA. All three point in the same direction. They provide a common answer to the riddle of right and wrong.

31   The Riddle Answered?

Have we done what we need to? Have we developed a comprehensive set of Principles for right and wrong that escapes the old problems? Do we have a system for making decisions we can *prove* is correct? The answers seem to be 'yes'!

In Chapter 5 we identified seven major problems with basing decisions on 'do whatever has the best consequences'. We have dealt with them all. This is how the new system for making decisions based on the Help Principle resolves each one:

1. *'Do whatever has the best consequences' can be self-defeating.* This is not a problem for the new system for making decisions because you cannot apply the Help Principle more by applying it less. When the best way to help someone is to withhold other forms of help, we just need to be careful what counts as 'help', and this was covered in Chapter 17. And we don't need to help someone intent on destroying the Help Principle because we can apply the reciprocity rule. This problem is solved.

2. *'Do whatever has the best consequences' only considers future consequences, ignoring important events in the past.* Past actions are now fully included, as they should be. All-time value tackles this problem. (For more on this, see Chapter 16.)

3. *'Do whatever has the best consequences' places decision-making authority in questionable hands.* We have removed this problem,

too. The Help Principle only looks at direct benefits to people; person-to-person wants have been excluded from our calculations. The Help Principle doesn't pander to their racism, favouritism, or any other –ism. (This was covered in Chapter 18.)

4. *'Do whatever has the best consequences' doesn't discriminate fairly between people.* The Help Principle is OK here, too. We have built up a system for making decisions based on individual people making individual decisions – people are no longer interchangeable. The Help Principle reconnects people with the value in their life, their own record of helping others in the past and what they deserve in the future. Problem solved.

5. *'Do whatever has the best consequences' sacrifices individual concerns to the group interest.* We have two solutions to this with our two rules for decision-making in small and large groups. In a small group, the individual wins through; in a large group, the group has the upper hand. Hence, the Help Principle finds a middle way between letting the group dominate the individual and letting the individual dominate the group – one which is sensitive to the needs of the individual and the size of the group. This was dealt with in Chapters 28 and 29.

6. *'Do whatever has the best consequences' downgrades promises, fairness and telling the truth.* We have applied the Help Principle to promises, fairness and truth-telling directly, and come out with clear answers which do not downgrade them at all. The Help Principle has produced definitive guidelines on when to lie, when to make promises and when to break them. We even have rules on fair punishments, mercy and remorse, from Chapters 23 to 26. Again, problem solved.

7. *'Do whatever has the best consequences' doesn't offer any clear rules.* Our new system has developed a very clear set of rules. These rules are set out in Chapter 30.

Perhaps the greatest triumph of the Help Principle is that there is a clear and independent reason to believe it (summarized in Chapter 14).

Whereas the beguiling logic underpinning 'do whatever has the best consequences' fell apart under scrutiny in Chapter 5, the reasons behind the Help Principle provide a firm foundation for a whole system for making decisions. Nor have we just formalized our intuitions and prejudices, although we have used them to guide us. We have identified a credible reason why we should do things, and used it to find answers to the outstanding problems of right and wrong.

The riddle of right and wrong is solved!

Or is it . . .?

Part V

Practical Advice: For Real People in the Modern World

32   So Why Aren't People Good, Then?

Utopia describes an ideal place. It is a world where everybody behaves as they should and everything works perfectly.

Many writers have tried to give shape to Utopia, suggesting what people should do to elevate the world from its everyday problems towards perfection. Plato described an elitist Utopia around 400BC. St Augustine wrote a Christian version 800 years later, placing the emphasis on religious worship. Karl Marx described Utopia as a class-less society which he believed could only emerge after a period of com-munist dictatorship. John Lennon imagined Utopia as a brotherhood of man with everybody 'living for today'. Each writer had their own view of what people should do. They all tried to show how, if everybody behaved properly, it could lead to perfection.

The word 'Utopia' comes from the title of a book written in 1516 by Thomas More. More's vision of ideal society described a faraway group of people who banished poverty by sharing their wealth. Aggression was rare, most people helped each other and few laws were needed because everybody knew what to do.

More's society is quite similar to what might emerge if everybody adopted the Help Principle. If most people followed the advice set out in Chapter 30 then they would help each other more. People would be lifted out of desperate poverty, emergencies would be tackled swiftly and dangers would be quenched decisively. The duty to intervene would make it harder for rogues to threaten others with harm, meaning there would be less aggression, violence and war. Meanwhile, people would work together to tackle the most important problems using the rules for deciding in groups, large and small. Diseases would be cured faster, the economy would work better, and the world's resources would be used properly. Overall, many more good decisions would be made. Just like More's 'Utopia', there would be less need for laws because everybody would know what to do.

But Thomas More's vision came with a cruel sting: the word 'Utopia' was created from the Greek words for 'not' and 'place' – 'Utopia' means somewhere that doesn't exist! Just as More's Utopian ideals were not taken up, the advice set out in Chapter 30 is not being applied either. War, poverty and disease are all too common. So, why don't people apply the Principles?

To explore the reasons, compare yourself with someone called Kintu who lives in Africa, whom you have never met. You are much, much richer than Kintu – he has to work hard in the fields every day just to survive. Several members of his extended family have already died of malnutrition, and his village suffers badly from a dirty water supply which has caused deaths from cholera and makes diarrhoea endemic, weakening the whole community to whatever other diseases emerge. Your money is worth much more to him than it is to you, and he would put any extra resources to very good use by fixing the water and sanitation system in the village. He is especially deserving of your help – indeed, Kintu is actually the most deserving person in the world: the single person who will make best use of the help you can offer him. If you applied the Help Principle, then you should give him a large portion of your income. But you don't. Why?

In Chapter 5 we could identify seven clear failings with Sven's system for making decisions, 'do whatever has the best consequences'. There seem to be another seven why the Principles that flow form the Help Principle are not in place, either:

1. *Information.* You don't know how hard Kintu works, or how much he's helped others in the past. You don't know how much help he

needs, or what sort of help. You don't know what would happen to the world economic system if everybody applied the Help Principle to people like Kintu. There is just too much to know, and some of it can never be known.

2. *Certainty.* Even if you did have some information about Kintu, how much could you trust it? If you send him some money, how do you know it would reach him? It's not just a question of information, but of having *reliable* information.

3. *Why him?* There are at least a billion people facing chronic poverty. Why not help one of the others instead?

4. *Who's responsible?* Why should it be you who helps Kintu – why not someone else? Surely there are people more responsible than you for helping Kintu.

5. *Your relative status.* If you did help Kintu, what would that mean for you in your own local community? People often judge themselves relative to others, and giving to Kintu when others do not means you would lose out in your neighbourly social competition.

6. *Your previous commitments.* Meanwhile, you have your own family to think about. You may have promised to help them, and honouring your promise means helping Kintu takes second place.

7. *Inertia.* Finally, the fact you have not helped Kintu in the past seems to provide a reason for not helping him now. Inertia means you act in the way you are used to acting. You don't challenge everything you do – that's too much to think about. So you tend to do what you've done before and behave as people expect you to behave.

So there are lots of reasons why you don't help Kintu. There are problems of information, certainty, deciding whom to help, diffuse responsibility, relative rather than absolute status, your other commitments and inertia. There may be other reasons too.

These problems do not just affect the Help Principle, but the other Principles also. It's difficult to know how much someone else has invested in your promises, so it is difficult to know whether it is right to break them. It's difficult to get information about other people's intentions, so it is difficult to judge people by them. It's difficult to help others with humility when you are concerned about your relative status, and so on.

Some small groups manage to avoid these difficulties. When you discipline your own children, for example, you might be sure who to discipline and who is to do the disciplining – the problems of relativity, overlapping commitments and inertia don't feature. In village communities these seven problems might emerge but still be manageable. In large, complex societies the problems can become so overwhelming that they prevent the Principles from being applied. Some anthropologists think the nature of a community can change abruptly when it has more than about 150 members. With more than this number, it's hard to keep track of your neighbours and how much help they need and deserve. Businesses, army units and schools all tend to develop internal rivalries when they have more than 150 people; some are deliberately split into subunits of less than 150 people to avoid this happening. In other words, all the problems of information, responsibility and the rest suddenly make it impractical to apply the Principles in communities with more than 150 members. When this happens, people tend to form a series of smaller communities – villages, families and networks of friends.

Although this means that the Principles can still be applied within each small community, the Principles tend not to be applied *between* people in different communities. Kintu, in a community in Africa, is denied the help he deserves because the people who should help him are too far away. Their help is worth more to Kintu than it is to themselves, but the community structure means they don't do what they should. It is a problem in the nature of the world: problems which conspire to prevent people applying the Principles.

It's as if the Principles no longer fit our real world, which is disconcerting, and should make us wonder what went wrong. The Principles were drawn up logically: if you accept we should seek value and that we need words like 'should' and 'ought' to seek it, then you have to accept the principles because they follow automatically – just as if you accept a shape has four straight sides of equal length and two are perpendicular, then you have to accept it is a square with four right-angled corners in total. You can even draw a square on a small sheet of paper, or on the ground, to prove it. But when you try to map out a much bigger square onto the Earth, you will find the corners are now greater than 90 degrees because the earth isn't flat. If you try to make the corners square, then the sides have to curve. Something has to give; our perfect square only works on a small scale. It doesn't quite fit on the imperfect Earth, and the principles don't quite fit either.

Nowadays, almost five hundred years since Thomas More's book, the concept of 'Utopia' is associated with naivety. Utopia doesn't just represent an impossible place; it's a place one has to be naive to pursue.

If the advice for right and wrong is to improve the world, there has to be a more practical way to apply it – one which withstands all the inevitable problems of information, certainty, diffuse responsibility, and so on. We still need to know what to do and how much to help people like Kintu. We can never create Utopia on a large scale, but we still need to know how to make our imperfect world as good as it can be.

33   Why People Hate Lawyers

Lawyers are some of the least popular people around. They seem to be trusted less than politicians, respected less than journalists and appreciated less than dentists. This unpopularity has several causes – perhaps lawyers are overpaid, perhaps some are nasty. But one of the main reasons is that people often feel cheated by them: they expect lawyers to do what is right, only to be disappointed.

Although some lawyers are excellent, the source of this disappointment is often lawyers themselves. Many deliberately try to make the law a litmus test for right and wrong – they imply their authority is moral, not just legal. Yet, for most people, the difference between legal and illegal doesn't turn on high principles. Instead, it turns on technicalities, obscure precedents and how much you pay. The profession has patented a version of 'justice' and auctions it to the highest bidder. No wonder lawyers are so often ridiculed.

The view that law defines right and wrong is very old. Absolute monarchies saw no distinction at all: kings were unquestionably right, and their words became law. The old French word 'droit' meant both 'law' and 'right' – they were the same. This link was broken by writers like John Austin, born soon after the French Revolution, who argued law-makers should make laws which maximized happiness; laws which didn't do this were wrong, therefore there could be a difference between legal justice and moral justice. In the 1960s, academics like HLA Hart agreed that law and right were different, but unlike Austin, saw no problem with them remaining separate. Hart said law-makers shouldn't try to frame laws which improved the world – instead, they should deliberately stay away from traditional notions of 'right' and 'wrong', which had implications for keeping law out of certain areas of life, such as sexual morality. A final view emerged later, promoted by people like Ronald Dworkin, who said that right and wrong can be deduced from a body of laws as a whole, which allows judges to have discretion in cases where the law isn't clear.

Having derived Principles for right and wrong, we are obliged to take a position in this debate, and the position is this: law has to be a compromise between what is right and what is possible. Law entirely detached from what is right is pure coercion – there is no good reason to obey it. But law cannot be exactly the same as what is right either, for all the practical problems explained in the previous chapter: problems of information, certainty, responsibility, and so on. Courts have to decide what happened, tackling an information problem; they have to assign guilt 'beyond all reasonable doubt', dealing with a problem of certainty; then they have to make someone responsible, even though responsibility may be complicated. Legal justice and real justice must overlap, but in our imperfect world they cannot be identical.

Chapter 30 set out what people should do when there were no problems with information, responsibility, and so on. Now we need to know what the law should command when these real-life nuisances are added in. And for this, we need to understand what laws are.

Laws are conventions: guidelines manufactured to influence what we do. Laws are the strongest sort of conventions, since they are backed up by threats of punishment. Other conventions, such as etiquettes, are weaker, enforced only by social approval and disapproval. The weakest conventions take the form of general advice, which carry no sanctions at all.

These conventions dominate our lives. Whenever people combine ideas of right and wrong with estimates of what they think will happen they are using conventions. These are the received wisdoms and vague generalities impressed on us in almost every social situation. If we were trying to project a square onto the curved surface of the earth, conventions would tell us whether it was more important go keep the sides straight or make the corners right-angled.

The best of these conventions help people to apply the Principles in the real world – they help to overcome all the problems set out in the previous chapter. For example, given the risk that people spread disease when they cough, the Help Principle would advise people to cover their mouths in most cases. But applying the Help Principle every time you cough involves a complex calculation on the risk of infecting others – it is much easier to tell people to cover their mouth *always* than it is to work out the chances of spreading the illness every few minutes. 'Cover your mouth when you cough' is a convention that simplifies an information problem which would otherwise make it very hard to apply the Principles.

Laws are conventions which can help overcome other obstacles to applying the Principles. Property laws can help ensure people get what they deserve. Tax laws can formalize people's obligation to help others; sentencing laws can set standards for the punishment of certain crimes, and so on. These conventions are rarely perfect replicas of the Principles for right and wrong. Sometimes they approximate to the Principles applied to a specific situation, like the etiquette to cover your mouth when you cough. Sometimes they are instrumental in helping the Principles be applied, as with conventions on property. There is nothing perfectly good about either covering your mouth or respecting property, but they both make good things more likely. So, we should *adopt conventions which help the Principles be applied, or approximate usefully to them.*

Unlike the Principles for right and wrong, conventions can conflict with each other. Should you respect the etiquette to eat rice with chopsticks, or respect a different convention to eat your food before it gets cold which requires switching to a spoon? Should you obey a convention not to walk on the grass, or break it to pick up some litter? There are plenty of difficult cases where people have to decide which convention to support and which to cast aside. Quandaries like this form the staple material for the 'agony aunts' who advise many magazine readers on tricky issues.

It is when conventions clash that many problems arise. It means that rather than provide clear answers to people, conventions are adding to the headache: not only do people have to resolve the issue at hand, they also have to decide which convention to break. Sometimes people can choose between clashing conventions by seeing which is most in line with the Help Principle. This can be easy – if you are forced to choose between a convention which advocates cannibalism and one which advocates being nice to strangers, you should clearly choose the latter. So, when one convention is way out of line with the Principles and it's easy to change, we should simply adopt new conventions which approximate to the Principles as much as possible, given the problems of information, certainty, and so on. But usually, when conventions clash, the choice is more complicated, and it can be complicated in one of two ways.

The first is when it's hard to decide how wrong the convention is. Consider the common convention that people should avoid oysters when there is no 'r' in the month. The convention has a sound basis: warm waters in May, June, July and August increase the risk of nasty bacteria in the seafood. Applying the rule is a useful shorthand, far easier than calculating risks each time you eat based on recent sea temperature, bacterial growth rates, and so on. But if there has been a particularly cold spring, it's a fair bet that early May oysters will be fine – so applying the convention means some safe oysters will be wasted. The trouble is you can't be sure, which is exactly why the 'r'-in-the-month convention was there in the first place. With cases like this, we need to apply a 'convention about conventions' – that is, an approximate rule which tells us when to change the conventions we follow.

The second situation when it is difficult to choose between conventions is when those conventions themselves have weight. Laws may be wrong, but we need to think twice before we break them. Like promises, we shouldn't break them whenever it suits us. Again, we need a convention about conventions, to tell us when we should break a law, and when we should obey it, despite its failings.

Conventions about conventions are most obvious in the legislation business: they are the constitutions and parliamentary practices that law-makers must respect. The convention about the convention on eating oysters is less obvious, but we can work out at least one important characteristic about it: if the spring was only a little colder than usual, we may well stick with the 'r'-in-the-month rule; but if we were in the southern hemisphere, where the months with an 'r' in them are cold, not warm, we would abandon the convention without hesitation. So conventions are specific to certain situations, where there is a pattern to what happens and we can induce what might happen in the future. Conventions lose their value when the pattern changes. Any convention about conventions must take this into account, even though changes in patterns can be hard to pinpoint: good oysters in early May could be a one-off, or they could indicate a long-term change in weather patterns which means we need to revise the 'r'-in-the-month rule – it takes time to tell.

The convention about conventions we should adopt seems to be this: *change conventions which depend on out-of-date patterns or situations* (e.g. oysters and weather patterns); *which can be refined easily; or which diverge substantially from the Principles* (e.g. cannibalism).

Deciding whether conventions need to change can be hard, especially when it involves a reality-check because checking with reality is difficult. It requires judgement – judgement about the state of the world. Not judgement about right and wrong themselves; they're clear now, and the people who argue right and wrong is all about judgement have misunderstood. The judgement part is now confined entirely to understanding how the world works, not how the world should be.

Most people get this judgement slightly wrong. We tend to assume a convention is still in place until it's obviously changed. This can be good: conventions rely on a sense of permanence to be effective and they wouldn't be able to do their magic if they were disposable. Indeed, breaking conventions is taboo for most people. But the trouble is that this magic keeps bad conventions alive, too, long after they should have been changed: it's good we wait for the red traffic light to change before we drive on, but if it stays red for 10 minutes it's probably broken and we should ignore the lights until they are fixed.

The convention about convention means some guidelines can never be perfected – and trying to perfect them can be self-defeating. For example, if every time you cough you try to calculate whether it really is worth raising your hand, you will be worse off than if you simply followed the convention to cover your mouth every time. Even though most conventions only *approximate* to the Principles, looking too hard for these flaws is a flaw in itself.

In practice, rather than choose between conventions, we tend to adjust them: 'don't eat oysters when there's an 'r' in the month' evolves into 'don't eat oysters when there's an 'r' in the month *in the northern hemisphere, when the weather's normal*'. In this way, our conventions can interbreed and adapt to the situations we find.

Conventions are organic: just as real DNA evolves into many competing life-forms, the DNA of right and wrong evolves, through conventions, into many different cultural codes, each suited to local problems of information, certainty, responsibility, and so on. Since these local problems can vary by place and time, different cultures can easily come up with different answers, and all of them can be correct. Because switching from a bad convention to a better one can be complicated and costly, and because different environments create different problems of information, certainty, and so on, there is no unique best set of conventions to adopt. Even trying to define the best conventions for a single culture is hard: it takes us away from the realm of right and wrong into psychology, organizational theory, economics, and so on. The Principles remain universal; their offspring are not universal at all.

So:

1. When there are no problems applying the Principles, we should apply them.

2. When there are problems – problems of information, diffuse responsibility, and so on – we should use conventions: guidelines manufactured to help overcome these problems.
3. Conventions can clash, providing contradictory advice. When this happens, we should choose between them on the basis of the Principles – which means applying the 'convention about conventions': we should change conventions based on out-of-date patterns or situations, which can be refined easily, or which diverge substantially from the Principles.
4. The convention about conventions means some flawed conventions are worth keeping, and that it can be right for two incompatible conventions to coexist at the same time.
5. Nevertheless, as practical problems change, conventions need to evolve and adapt accordingly. We should challenge conventions which no longer help people apply the Principles for right and wrong in the situation they face. Conventions are rarely perfect, and we should be ready to disobey them from time to time.

Applying these five steps to society provides an agenda for social evolution. The etiquettes which guide us need to change as the world changes around us. We have an obligation to make sure these etiquettes adapt as they should, which means we should all challenge certain assumptions about appropriate behaviour.

Applying these five steps to the law means there will be times when laws need to be amended, when civil obedience is justified and when we should challenge the sanctity of the courtroom. Usually we should only do this in line with due process – respecting the convention about conventions. But even these constitutional conventions can be wrong. Sometimes, occasionally, the law is wrong and we should break it. Lawyers who refuse to accept this because they have come to believe their system of justice defines right and wrong deserve to be unpopular.

34   When It's Best to Be Bad

We have already found flaws in several common conventions, such as those on lying, promises and majority rule. Now we will look at one of the most fundamental conventions of all: the notion we should make sure our individual actions are always good. This is personal integrity, and it is about doing what's right yourself, keeping *your* hands clean, whatever happens around you.

Consider fair-trade coffee, for example. This guarantees coffee farmers a reasonable price for their crop and allows consumers to know they are helping someone far away; unlike coffee brought to market by some conglomerates, fair-trade growers earn enough to make a sustainable livelihood from their work. People can buy fair-trade coffee and know their actions are pure, even if other consumers' are not. The supermarkets which sell fair-trade coffee offer, in turn, more than just the product – they also sell the right to be smug. People can pick it off the shelves, walk passed underpaid staff to the checkout where they also buy products made in sweatshops and still feel good about themselves. In the isolating worlds of television and supermarkets where people can watch, listen and buy without interacting with anybody else, it is easy for right and wrong to become purely individualized concepts, something to be picked up in a shopping aisle. As long as *you* do what's right, that's all that matters.

This approach owes much to the Stoics of the Roman era who detached themselves from the chaos around them as their ancient empire collapsed. Inspired by the writings of Emperor Marcus Aurelius, the Stoics became steadfast and self-reliant, locating virtue purely in their own actions. Some religions also teach right and wrong as purely a list of personal actions, and claim that taking responsibility for one's own actions is *all* morality is about. It is a controversial idea: critics say being good is a social concept, so trying to be 'good' without considering other people is nonsense.

Personal integrity – make sure you do the right thing whatever else is happening – is a convention, alongside the conventions of laws and etiquette. It is a convention which Sven decided to ignore when he took Erik's place in the torture chamber, judging that reducing suffering was more important than this popular principle. The philosopher Bernard Williams has challenged the logic which encourages Sven to take the job. Personal integrity means something to Williams – can he persuade Sven to change his mind?

Williams's first attempt to dissuade Sven would appeal to his own life plan: does Sven really want to spend his life working in a torture chamber? Sven is the sort of person who has always wanted to work hard at whatever he does. It would be a major sacrifice for him to take the senior position with the internal police service, where he knows the best thing to do is to be a slacker. Sven can never get any public respect if he subverts the police service from the inside, which is an added irritant for someone who's always thrived on public recognition.

Sven might be tempted by this argument, but he should reject it: this is just selfish vanity portrayed in a more positive light. Seeking public respect is easily dismissed: the rule on humility says that Sven should not demand rewards or praise for his efforts. Wanting a wholesome life plan and wanting to work hard are trickier because they are *usually* good. But Sven must remember why these things are usually good, and realize they are not good now. It would be a mistake to think these things had intrinsic value.

Second, Williams might encourage Sven to be honest: if he takes the senior position with the brutal interior police he will have to sign a contract of employment and promise to work his hardest. Of course, it is a promise Sven intends to break, but that is the complication: Sven is a generally honest person who doesn't like making false promises.

Sven may well be nervous about signing the contract because it will involve promising to work hard when really he will try to subvert the institution. But the Help Principle provides rules for when to make promises and when to break them, and this time Sven should sign the employment contract with his fingers crossed. His qualms over signing without sincerity are groundless. Again, Sven needs to understand the reason for being honest, realize it doesn't apply here, and accept he shouldn't be honest just for the sake of it.

Williams' third and final argument would query exactly what good Sven expects to do by joining the brutal police service. He will still have to torture people, even if he does it more kindly than Erik would have done. If he became a teacher instead, the impact of his good work would be much more obvious. So why not become a teacher?

Sven will certainly be detached from the good consequences of his actions in the torture chamber. It will take some imagination to think about the bad things he prevents Erik from doing, but he does need to consider them. It would be short-sighted for Sven to rate the first-hand good he can do as a teacher as more important than the distant but greater good he can do in the torture chamber. There is no good reason for Sven to downgrade the consequences which are more detached from him. He should count all the consequences of his actions.

So there are three reasons why Williams may be able to make him uneasy about his choice. There is Sven's life plan to do something he values (he doesn't value working for the interior police); his respect for promises (he doesn't want to sign an employment contract he won't uphold); and a problem of detached consequences (Sven is far away from the good consequences of his actions). Williams can show that by rejecting the convention on personal integrity, Sven would also be rejecting conventions on living a wholesome life, keeping promises and doing good first-hand.

But Sven can answer that these three conventions are just like the convention on personal integrity: there are *usually* good reasons for them but they don't apply now. Sticking to these outmoded conventions would be like refusing oysters in June while living in Australia.

The convention on personal integrity is deeply embedded within most of us. We all feel uneasy when we do bad things, and usually we should. But there are several times when it's best to be bad. We should be bad when being good is worse because of the way our actions can influence the behaviour of others.

This has three important implications.

First, we must try hard to see the full consequences of our actions. Just as it was hard for Sven to think about the innocent torture victims he was saving from Erik's brutality, it is often hard for us to think about the people faraway who we decide not to help when we decide to do something else. We should never give too much praise to someone who makes a small detour to help someone else – think of all the other people they could have helped but didn't. Seeing the full consequences of our actions is difficult, sometimes verging on the impossible, and for actions with consequences beyond the cloudy fringe of our predictive powers we have no choice but to interpret our actions narrowly – if Sven doubts someone nasty would replace him then he should have doubts about taking the job. But although we cannot see everything, we should always try to see as far ahead as we can.

Second, we need to see beyond the most obvious calls for help and remember the less obvious ones. Some charities ask us to help cuddly animals with sympathetic eyes. These images implore us to give, but we should not let their emotive appeal distort our priorities. Some of the things we need to do may be less compelling but more important.

And third, in an imperfect world, when we are forced to compromise with our personal integrity, we still need to think of ways of making the world better. Sven still has a duty to try to overthrow the regime. You can do what's bad to stop other people doing something worse, but you should still try to do what's best.

Out goes personal integrity. It can be good to be bad; two wrongs *can* make a right. But before Stoics shriek in horror, they should realize there is a more profound sort of integrity which we must adopt instead: that the *integrity* of what we cause to happen has good effects. We have not abandoned the Stoic concept of personal responsibility; we have filled it out to include some important factors that the Stoics ignored. Indeed, perhaps we can see where the Stoics were coming from. When uncertainty increases, as it did in the dying days of the Roman Empire and perhaps now too, the actions of other people can become harder to predict, meaning the direct effects of our own actions become more important. The Stoic position coincides with the best thing to do when everything is crashing down around you.

So, we should usually buy fair-trade coffee, refuse to work for nasty regimes and make sure we do the right thing. But whenever our actions alter what other people do, we may have to do things differently. To be specific, we should *do bad things only when the behaviour of others means any better actions will have worse effects*. Whenever these situations arise, we must never forget our other duty – to try to remove the causes of the problem. We should abandon personal integrity only when something greater is at stake; and when we do, we must try to address the root causes. A world in which it's best for everybody to do what's best is better than the twisted, complicated world of today, where doing something bad can sometimes be the best thing to do.

35   The Live Aid Problem: Does Charity Begin at Home?

On 13 July 1985, 160,000 people gathered at stadiums in London and Philadelphia to witness one of the greatest ever rock events. 'Live Aid' featured some of the best acts of the time and was described as a 'global jukebox'. Sixteen hours of music was televised worldwide attracting an audience of 1.5 billion people.

The event was held to raise funds for people dying of famine in Ethiopia. Emotive videos of starving children were broadcast between the live entertainment, compelling people to donate cash. Bob Geldof, who helped organize the event, famously demanded 'People are dying NOW. Give us the money NOW. Give me the money now.' Some £150 million was raised, enabling a massive life-saving relief effort in East Africa.

The basic Help Principle – help someone if your help is worth more to them than it is to you – creates a clear imperative to help starving people when we have food ourselves, and Live Aid made people act on this. Some argue charity begins at home; Live Aid answered that charity was more vital elsewhere. But it was a one-off occasion – we cannot pin all our hopes on extraordinary rock concerts, and, sadly, most starving people cannot survive until the next one.

Most cultures have very deeply ingrained codes about the importance of helping those close to us, especially spouses and blood relations. Indeed, listening to some accounts of right and wrong, it is easy to imagine that being good amounts to little more than being good to your family. Cultures disagree on exactly how important family is: some say we have a duty to help a nephew get on in their career while others regard it as nepotism, but all have conventions which say families deserve something extra. Special relationships deserve special treatment. If we abandoned our own children to help children far away we would not be seen as a good person. Indeed, people who actually make no distinction between friends and strangers endanger their whole well-being. Close relationships make up the essence of life. Altruism to strangers needs to be tempered with the empathy of good, close personal relations.

But we can't put friends and relatives first simply because we prefer to help them; helping people simply on the basis of who you want to help is very selfish. Empathy and obligation are impartial between friends and strangers too; the DNA of right and wrong is strictly neutral – we should show as much kindness to strangers as we do to friends. We need to decide how important our special relationships should be, and how much we should rate friends above strangers. To draw out your instincts on this, imagine seeing lots of people struggling in deep water. You worry some may drown. It would be natural to try to save your spouse rather than someone else, but should you put the life of your husband or wife before the lives of two strangers? Or three? Or ten?

When someone you know is in trouble, you may be able to help them more than other people. You might be able to empathize with them more, and the more you understand their interests the more valuable your help will be. Sometimes there is an extra reason to help those closest to you because there is a clear understanding that it is *your* responsibility to look after a family member, just as it is other people's responsibility to look after someone else. Both of these reasons apply to children: we have a clear responsibility to look after them, and we all, in effect, promise we will put our own children first. Societies enshrine these promises as conventions, sometimes called the duty of care.

Do all promises made in the past justify preferential treatment? Wedding vows, in which each spouse promises preferential treatment to their partner, are common to most cultures. We wouldn't query someone who tried to save their wife or husband before they saved someone else's. But if someone promised a racist fraternity to put white people first and then tried to save only white people when lots of others were drowning, we would disapprove. We respect some promises to offer preferential treatment but not others.

We can sort good promises from bad by referring to what we have already deduced about promises: they should be made only if the certainty they instil is worth more than the best option they rule out. This makes a promise to put your own child first a 'good' promise – it brings benefits like making them more relaxed in the playground. Promises to look after your own children are useful in society – they help allocate responsibility, and ensure the Help Principle is applied. If several children fall off the climbing frame at the same time, then there is a case for going to your child before you go to other people's. Only if someone else's child is significantly worse off should you put your promise aside and help the other child first. 'Bad' promises are different, such as the promise made by the racist to help only white children, because they serve no good purpose.

All this means there are two justifications for putting friends and relatives before strangers, but both are limited. First, you *can* put friends and relatives first if you understand them better than you understand other people, so you can help them more. Second, preferential treatment can be justified by promises, but these promises only count if they enable the Help Principle to be applied more generally.

So, we *should* have special relationships with friends and family, but these only allow a limited amount of preferential treatment. It's no good ignoring Live Aid because you give all your time to your children. We still need to help people we don't know, especially if they need our help much more than our friends and family. When we see our spouse among several strangers struggling in the water we should go to our wife or husband first, but the lives of the others should come before their comfort. As a rule, we should *distribute our help to others according to their different needs, how much we can help each of them, and any fair promises we have made.* Special relationships can dull our duties to everybody else but never obscure them.

This is where the most serious problems begin. If we say people should rate the concerns of strangers almost as highly as those of friends and family, then there are suddenly many more people to think about. You may have eight close family members, eighty good friends and eight hundred acquaintances, all of whom you would help in varying degrees, but there are many millions of Kintus in the world and a billion people living on less than a dollar a day. Live Aid set an example of helping millions of people in desperate need of help – the ideal embodiment of the Help Principle in some ways. But now it seems we should spread our help to others so thinly the only obvious effect of giving will be to make each of us poorer. We have lost our limits and need to find them again. This is the greatest practical problem of right and wrong, and this is the problem we shall now tackle.

36 The Mother Teresa Quandary: Can You Be Good without Giving Everything Away?

A few people have accepted the daunting obligation to help everybody. People like Mother Teresa, who was born in 1910 in Skopje, but devoted most of her life to helping poor people in Calcutta, India. From 1950 onwards, Teresa established charity centres to care for the 'poorest of the poor', inspiring a network which had reached more than half the countries in the world by the time she died, in 1997. She was widely (though not universally) admired, and some people believe she personified selflessness: she seemed to help others without any regard to herself. People like Mother Teresa are extremely rare: she really did place herself on an equal level with the very poorest people in society. She would deprive herself to cater for people in deprivation, no matter how many there were.

Mother Teresa presents a quandary for everybody who wants to be good. She seemed to live the perfect life, yet it was a life which very few of us feel able to copy. If this is true, then it means very few people can really be good. The rest of us have to cower in our flaw-ridden selves and abandon the dream of doing what is right. Mother Teresa's example condemns the rest of us to being bad people.

Fortunately, this logic is mistaken; being good is not out of reach. But to see why, we need to follow the argument through in more detail.

Imagine you are rich in a poor country and you applied the basic Help Principle in full to everybody you met. You might give almost half your wealth to the first extremely poor person you met. The next person you met would then receive almost half of what was left, and so on. If you met just ten very poor people and applied the Help Principle to each one in turn, you could end up ten *thousand* times poorer.

This is just too much to ask of people, including most who advocate a fairer society. From rich superstars to middle-income people with a conscience, the recognition we need to do something about poverty is far more common than the sort of self-depriving selflessness demonstrated by Mother Teresa. Indeed, the fact so many people call for poverty to end but refuse to take the lead themselves has left some open to the charge of hypocrisy. In most cases it is not quite that but sometimes it comes close.

Several cultures have already developed conventions on how much we should help others. These conventions provide the limits we need and, as long as people are content no further charity is needed, they provide robust immunity to hypocrisy, too. Islam, Christianity, and several early tax systems converged on a common answer: they all advised people to devote one-tenth of their income to other people. The one-tenth model has proven to be sustainable over long periods, and with good local organizations it can ensure resources are channelled where they are most needed. But one-tenth seems arbitrary; the Gods who chose it could have decreed one-twelfth or one-eighth just as easily. Also, one-tenth seems awkward in a modern age when governments already take much more than one-tenth of income as tax and use some of it for charitable purposes. And, like all conventions, it only works while a certain pattern holds – in this case, a pattern of needs within the community. When the community changes or faces a crisis, one-tenth may be too much or too little. We cannot have faith that one-tenth is the limit we need.

We can find the right limit if we apply the Help Principle more carefully. Imagine you are in a supermarket car park loading up your vehicle before you drive away. You notice an old woman struggling with her bags; helping her with her bags is worth more to her than the small distraction it costs you, so you help her. While you are doing so, another shopper, also infirm and needing assistance, comes over and asks for you to do the same for him. Again, the Help Principle applies, so you help him. Then you are approached by a third shopper, and a fourth, and you help each one in turn. You begin to wonder whether you will ever escape the car park . . .

Repeating the Help Principle in this way suggests you should help each person who comes along, even if it transforms you into a permanent car park attendant. But this logic is flawed. Since the impact of all these acts of charity falls on the same person – you – you can consider their cumulative impact, and something like the rule for decision-making in small groups applies. Even though your help is worth more to each shopper than it is to you, there is a limit after, say, the fourth person, when your actions to *all* the other shoppers are actually causing you more problems than the benefits you are bringing each one. At this point you are entitled to drive away or recruit others to take your place. You may feel bad seeing people still struggling with their bags as you leave, but can be satisfied you have done enough.

It's the same with poverty. We know there are people like Kintu who desperately need our help, and when Kintu dies of malnutrition or disease there will be another Kintu just the same since there are about a billion people in situations almost as dire as his; many of them are children, and six thousand of these are dying from diarrhoea every day. They need help to survive, not to just load their shopping, but like the people in the car park there is still a limit to the total amount of help any individual should give. The limit is determined by how much help they need, how much you and others can help them, and, indeed, how many of them there are. We can work out how much we should help each one and, like helping the shoppers, our obligations are manageable.

So we don't have to give everything away, like Mother Teresa. We can still be good without giving away every precious thing we have. The Mother Teresa quandary has been solved.

More importantly, we can establish better conventions on how much we should help others – it *is* possible to deduce exactly how much we should help others, including how much we need to do about the appalling numbers of people dying from diarrhoea, and this is what we will do in the next chapter.

37 The Man on the Morning Train

A man rides the morning train to work. He looks out of the window at the houses and wonders about the lives of people who live in them. He looks at the other commuters, and wonders what they all do.

There is an unspoken rule on the train that the passengers don't talk to each other. Indeed, they barely interact at all. There seems to be a convention that each person is their own best guardian; they don't need to help each other, and it would be counter-productive if they tried. They would just disturb each other. But the man on the morning train worries this convention is too widespread. He knows about lethal poverty abroad and wants to do more; trusting in the convention people should look after themselves doesn't seem right when people like Kintu don't have the basics needed to survive. He is thousands of miles from Kintu and he doesn't know how to help or how much he should do himself, but the man on the morning train wants to do what's right.

He is perplexed about all reasons not to help people in Africa: it is expensive and risky; poverty seems just too big a problem to tackle; he feels a stronger duty to people close to him; the economic system depends on people making decisions based on self-interest rather than charity; helping people like Kintu could make them dependent or lazy; and he feels his salary compensates him for the hard work he puts in, so he shouldn't give it to someone else. Then there are the everyday demands on his money: he earns a reasonable amount – twice the national average salary in a rich European nation. But one third of his earnings go in tax, another third pays his mortgage and the rest of his money is split between food, clothes, utility bills, his car, the occasional trip to his elderly parents, the costs of his young son, repaying student debts and, of course, his train ticket. There is hardly anything left over. He would have to change his life quite considerably to give just a few percent of his income away. He admires Mother Teresa but he can't afford to copy her.

Someone in a charity sweat shirt confronts him when he leaves the train, rattling a plastic jar and asking for money. He feels any donation will make virtually no impact on people like Kintu, so he swerves away from the charity collector, pretending to have missed them as he walks past. It leaves him feeling guilty and confused, but he is determined to work out what he should do.

The next day when he rides the train he looks again at the houses as he travels past them and counts the other passengers. There are almost thirty of them, just a few of the 6.8 billion people in the world. He should apply the Help Principle to each one of those 6.8 billion. But that number is too huge to understand properly, and 6.8 billion people are far too many people to know. To know how much he should help others he needs short cuts.

The first short cut comes from the reciprocity rule, which says he should only help those who would help others in turn. Perhaps a billion of the 6.8 billion will be selfish, so he can ignore them. And because he will only help people who reciprocate, it means he can work on the basis of the rule for choosing in groups with reciprocity: he should do whatever helps any person the most. That person is Kintu: helping him will save his life.

But Kintu doesn't need simple cash – there's nothing in his village to buy with it. He needs development, which means an investment programme for communities like his. Credible experts reckon the most important investments are in agriculture, health, education, power, transport, communication, water and sanitation. The total cost needed to help the billion Kintu's in the world, both rural and urban, is about $150 billion a year for 10 years, several thousand times the total amount raised by Live Aid in 1985. This will enable the UN Millennium Development Goals to be met and mean the world's richest countries will live up to the commitments they've already made to end extreme poverty worldwide.

How much of this $150 billion should be paid by the man on the morning train? Just as he can decide who to help on the basis of 'help whoever benefits the most', contributions should come from 'whoever will miss them the least'. This means billionaires should make the largest contributions, following the examples set by philanthropists like Bill Gates, Warren Buffett and George Soros. But others should contribute too, including the man on the morning train.

Calculating how much this man should contribute goes to the heart of the problem. If everybody in the world applied the Help Principle to everybody else, then there would be only four reasons why people had different levels of wealth: because they had worked harder than others; because they needed things more; because transferring resources would diminish the value of help given; and because of voluntary gambles. We can ignore voluntary gambles because of the autonomy principle – if people want to take a chance on becoming richer or poorer that is up to them. That means we should only be concerned by the first three: efforts invested, benefits to be had and problems transferring wealth between people.

Now we need to make some assumptions because getting exact information on billions of people is too difficult. We can assume the more money people have the less they need each extra unit of currency. Also, we can assume most people need roughly the same total amount of things. This suggests people should contribute a similar proportion of their wealth. When you do the sums on $150 billion, people should contribute about three-quarters of 1 per cent of their income to pro-grammes tackling lethal poverty. For the man on the morning train, this means $750 of his $100,000 each year. Roughly a third of this contri-bution is already being made on his behalf by the government, paid through his taxes, so he needs to give an extra $500.

He should make this contribution in whichever way hurts him least. That may mean making savings somewhere, lending his skills, or doing both. He should channel these resources in the most effective way possible, which probably means giving it through a respectable charity. He can delay giving now if it enables him to give more later, but he should not postpone it forever.

That leaves three remaining queries. First, although the man on the morning train is giving his fair share of the funds needed for people like Kintu, most others are not and the problems faced by people like Kintu will not be solved. To get others to pay their share, the man on the train could reciprocate their lack of good will. He would be entitled to give smaller Christmas presents to relatives who do not make a contribution, for example. More promising is, every time someone tells him he 'should' do something, to ask whether they have made their contribution to help people like Kintu, which is the most pressing 'should' of all; if not, then he should explain that their instructions are empty, since they have not followed them where they lead themselves. He should vote for politicians who will make the extra investment needed, and buy from companies which contribute to the anti-poverty programme too.

Second, he must remember his special relationships with friends and family. These continue. He should filter out any commitments to help others not rooted in good promises, so if he hires a new employee he shouldn't bias the process in favour of friends. But generally he will continue to offer a support network for friends and family as they offer support to him in return.

And third, he must remember all the other people in the world. These people are not facing lethal poverty, he doesn't know them and getting to know them individually will distract him more than any good which may result. There may be some forms of common aid which will benefit most of them – ending export subsidies will help most people in middle-income countries, so he could press his government to do that; he may be able to play his part on common problems, like climate change; and if he has a talent which will benefit many people then he should use it. Also, if a specific need arises, such as one of the other commuters on the morning train having a heart attack, then he should offer emergency first aid. But for most of these billions of people most of the time, trying to provide direct help will be counter-productive. The best the man on the train can do for these people is to uphold the convention that they should provide for themselves; they may need local or family support networks sometimes, but they don't need him to interfere at the moment.

He may wonder whether he has drawn the limit in the right place: he is actively supporting a billion Kintus to meet the Millennium Development Goals while actively deciding to let some five billion others fend for themselves. These five billion do not face lethal poverty but many are still seriously poor and his money will still be worth much more to them than it is to him. The problem, though, is getting it to them in a way that's useful. These people need reliable trading arrangements and trustworthy institutions much more than they need hand-outs. Hand-outs may even undermine the convention that they should provide for themselves – a convention which is generally good for these people even though it threatens to be fatal to Kintu. When the man on the train studies the much-disputed evidence on how effective aid is, he will probably confirm this conclusion (and if the evidence suggests aid is more or less effective, then he should help more or fewer people accordingly). The right and wrong part of what he should do has been sorted out; determining facts is all that remains.

When the man rides the evening train home he is comfortable with himself. He knows what to do for the people in the houses he travels past, he knows what to do for the other commuters, and he knows what to do for Kintu in Africa. He will donate to charity, persuade others to do the same and know he has done what is right. He knows the fair share he needs to contribute to address this common problem – he can apply the same method to work out his fair share to other common problems and encourage others to contribute to them too. All he needs now are the facts. The train ride will never be the same again.

38 How to Lead a Good Life in a Rough World

Chapter 30 set out advice for perfect situations. But this advice is too perfect for many real-life situations, where problems prevent us doing what's best. There are problems of information, certainty, knowing who you should help and who should help you, problems of relative rather than absolute status, previous commitments and inertia. These problems mean we need to adapt how we apply the Principles, and this is where conventions come in. Conventions give advice for real-life situations, and the best conventions make it easier to apply the Principles. But sometimes these conventions fail, as with the amount we should give to help people like Kintu. Sometimes they are misunderstood, as with personal integrity. Sometimes they are given too much or too little weight, as with conventions on families. Sometimes they are confused with what is right, as with the law. We need to adjust these conventions when the situations which gave rise to them change, and sometimes we need to break them outright.

Here is a summary of what we should do in our rough world. It is not a comprehensive list – for that, we would need to address many more of the specific problems people suffer, and these change from place to place and time to time. But it does set out some general guidance for developing good conventions in most situations. (Numbering starts from fifteen, so this list can be added to the fourteen points we've worked out already.)

15. *Give three-quarters of 1 per cent of your income to tackle lethal poverty.* Preventable deaths because people lack the basic resources needed to survive are our most desperate problem. We have a duty to prevent these deaths just as we have a duty to prevent murder, and our response should be shaped by what we can do. Three-quarters of 1 per cent of the income from everybody above the poverty line in the developed world is enough to tackle lethal poverty and stop six thousand children dying every day from diarrhoea.

16. *Contribute your fair share to solve common problems and encourage others to contribute their fair share too.* If someone is not contributing their share to tackle the world's most pressing problems then it undermines anything else they call for, and this should be explained to them. If they don't think they ought to help people like Kintu, then we can reciprocate their selfishness to them.

    This piece of guidance means we should press institutions to straighten their priorities. Governments and businesses have a role in tackling lethal poverty. We should switch our votes and purchases towards institutions which act in line with the Principles and related conventions. Once lethal poverty has been tackled, these institutions should tackle other vital issues, especially those with the largest consequences where we can have the greatest impact.

17. *Help people more if you know them or you owe them.* There are good reasons to put friends and family first: we usually understand their needs well and we may have important commitments to them which we should honour. But there is a limit to this preferential treatment, and the serious needs of strangers should always come before the petty needs of people we know.

18. *Respect good conventions and challenge bad ones.* To overcome the problems with applying the Principles, we should adopt conventions which approximate to the Principles or help them to apply. Different societies have developed different sets of conventions, and it is possible for two different sets of conventions to be right at the same time – we should usually respect foreign cultures, tolerate

different approaches and be aware that their answers may be better than ours because they have adapted to local circumstances. We should support conventions which help the Principles to be applied, even though this may mean adopting some conventions which seem to contradict each other.

Most people are too traditional which means many conventions last longer than they should. When conventions, at home or abroad, depend on out-of-date patterns or situations, can be refined easily, or diverge substantially from the Principles, then we should challenge them and try to make them better.

19. *Check your actions against your instincts; check your instincts are right for your situation.* When information is unreliable, as so often in life, our instincts can prevent us going drastically off course. But our instincts tend to mislead us too. They tend to be short-sighted, exaggerating the immediate effects of what we do at the expense of more distant consequences. They can also fool us into thinking conventions are valuable in themselves, not for their power to promote good, meaning we often stick with conventions when the situation has changed and they are no longer appropriate. We need reasoning to correct our instinctive response, and instincts to humanize our calculations.

20. *Only do bad things to stop other people doing worse.* It is naïve to think that keeping our own hands clean makes us good people – often it does, but it can also licence other people to be bad. By doing something bad we can sometimes stop other people doing something worse – two wrongs *can* make a right. When this happens, we should always seek a way of improving the whole system, so we don't have to be bad any more.

In general, we can often defeat the problems which stop people acting as they should. Where there is a problem with information, we can let people know. Where there is a problem of certainty, we can offer guarantees. Where there is a problem of responsibility, we can put someone in charge. For many of these solutions, and to establish the best conventions, we often need to act together. Social problems require social solutions. What these social solutions should be is for another time, but we aren't powerless until then – there are appropriate responses for individuals, too. Acting together and alone, we *can* improve this rough world. We *can* make the world a better place, so we should do so.

Part VI

The Prognosis: How to Make Good Decisions and Be Right All the Time

39   Newton's Limits

At last, we have answers we need. Finally, we know what we should do.

We have answers to all three problems set out at the beginning. We know what Sven should do. He was wondering whether to join the brutal interior police or allow cruel Erik to take his place. Now we know Sven *should* take up the position – it would be a selfish vanity for him to refuse to dirty his hands. And as he does something bad to stop other people doing worse, he must remember his wider objective of toppling the dictator's nasty regime.

We know what Sue should do. She was wondering whether to go to the dance with John as she had promised, or take up a new and more appealing invitation from Steve. What she should do depends on how much of a commitment she made to John and how much she prefers Steve. And if she doesn't think John will respond appropriately when told the truth about why she changed her mind, then Sue has a reason to lie to John when she turns down his invitation.

And we know what we should do about the six thousand people dying every day of diarrhoea. We know we should give considerable amounts of our time and money to stop them dying. We can calculate how much; it includes roughly three-quarters of 1 per cent of our income. And we know we should work with governments, charities, businesses and other institutions to make sure others contribute too, and that our help brings maximum benefits to people. People like Kintu in Africa *do* deserve our help and we should help them.

What is special about this advice is that it is more than advice. These are the Right Answers. They are not just matters of opinion; they are true.

We know these answers are right because of where they come from. These answers arise from a chain of thinking that goes right back to the meaning of life itself, to the DNA of right and wrong, and to the Principles which grow from them. If you disagree with these answers – if you think, for example, that Sven should turn down the job and let Erik work for the police – then you have to show some fault in that chain of thinking or in the way it has been applied in the particular case. Unless you can identify such a fault, then there is a fault in your own thinking.

Ultimately, what we should do derives from just two things: what we want, and trying to reconcile it with what other people want. It is no coincidence that most people's sense of right and wrong develops when they are children, as they come to interact with other children in the playground for the first time. Children soon start using terms like 'should', 'ought' and 'good', and with them, they understand the basic requirement that right and wrong must not contradict each other in certain ways if they are to motivate. With this, and a little knowledge of their surroundings, they can start to do what's best in their immediate world. They can make and break promises, they can understand punishments, and, when they share their toys with other infants, they can act on the Help Principle. Right and wrong may be complicated sometimes, but their origins are simple.

The set of Principles we have deduced also refine today's dominant ethical theory, the idea we should do whatever has the best consequences. The Help Principle incorporates all the good points of the theory without any of the bad points, providing a new system for making decisions. And it is a very versatile system which can give guidance on law, politics, romance, economics and many other fields, bringing these different strands of thinking into a single coherent whole. Finally, we have the system for making decisions we need.

Mystery has gone out of right and wrong. Just as science explains the natural world, we can now explain the world of what we should do. God is no longer needed to tell us what to do, and we don't need to rely on guesswork. We know.

Here, though, there is a problem – a problem shared with science. About a hundred years ago, two centuries after Newton, several scientists reported some odd results which didn't quite fit with Newton's formulae. When a measuring error was ruled out, it took the German genius Albert Einstein to explain where the mistake lay, and it was with Newton: his formulae didn't work on a very large scale. Some decades later, another German physicist, Werner Heisenberg, proved that if you know where a certain minuscule particle is, you can never be absolutely sure how fast it's travelling. His conclusion has since been known as the 'Heisenberg Uncertainty Principle', and it means Newton's laws don't work properly when they are applied at the tiniest scale, either. Einstein urged the Americans to develop the atomic bomb, while Heisenberg kept some of his nuclear work secret from the Nazis to stop them making one first. They both succeeded, but they had also exploded one of the founding certainties about how the world worked. After being understood for several centuries, movement was once again a mystery.

Away from the massive scales considered by Einstein and the minute scale studied by Heisenberg, we can see the limits of science in our everyday experience. We cannot always predict things even when science allows us to understand how they work. The weather, for example, is just too complex to forecast a month in advance. Even if we had all the weather balloons, thermometers and barometers we needed, and a supercomputer to process the abundant information they produced, calculating next month's weather would still be too complex for us. If we tried, all these devices would themselves influence what the weather would be like. Hence, we can never predict next month's weather perfectly. We can be reasonably sure summer months will be warmer than winter ones and that high atmospheric pressure will mean less wind, but our perfect understanding cannot give us perfect knowledge.

The same is true of right and wrong. Some situations are just too complex for us to know exactly what we should do. Delving inside some scenarios might help but then, like the weather balloons, our scrutiny would change the very thing we were trying to measure. Even though we have a thorough understanding of right and wrong, it doesn't mean we always know exactly what to do. We can make good decisions and be right, but we cannot know how to make good decisions and be right *all the time*.

This is where judgement re-enters the field. Because our situations are inherently uncertain, knowing what to do *can* involve judgement and wisdom. It involves understanding human character, a sense of how the world works and a realistic assessment of what is possible. In large modern societies, there are just too many things to calculate. To know what to do, you have to think in terms of broad trends, assumptions and generalities. We cannot displace judgement from the way things interact because the world is inherently unpredictable. And when we cannot see the world around us clearly, black-and-white decision-making fades to grey.

The problems in the world – problems of information, certainty, diffuse responsibility, and so on – force us to rely on conventions which can never be perfect because they echo the imperfections around us. When these conventions clash with each other we have a moral dilemma or, worse, a collision between different cultures. All our moral dilemmas and culture wars could be solved if we could drop the conventions and move back to the Principles, but that requires perfect knowledge of a situation, which is too hard to come by. Sometimes one culture is right and the other is wrong, but more often both cultures are right because their conventions evolved for different situations. The Principles of right and wrong are absolute and we should defend them, but different societies can turn them into different conventions in neighbouring valleys, and live that way for many generations. Neither should try to impose their conventions on the other.

All the disputes in life, all the moral dilemmas and all the confusion: these do not arise from any mystery over right and wrong. They arise from our imperfect understanding of the world. We can decode the DNA of right and wrong – this book sets out the genetic blueprint – but this is not enough to predict the life-form of every convention which will evolve. It is the mysteries of complex societies, the enigma of human emotions and uncertainty of the future which is the problem. And these are all mysteries about the movement of physical things – sometimes on a tiny scale, sometimes interacting with each other in a way too complicated to calculate, but they are all physical. We need a new set of physical laws to upgrade those derived by Newton. It is the final irony in our search for right and wrong: the formulae set out by Newton upon which we have modelled our goal are the very reason our goal cannot be achieved. The limits of Newton's Science set the limits for knowing right and wrong.

This means we need to think carefully before we accept advice. Most of the conventions a society adopts will be flawed in some way – that includes most of the institutions, most of the conventions about things like family and nationality, and most of the norms we are obliged to respect. Because all these things are imperfect we need to hesitate before we follow them. Constantly we need to check our society is not going drastically off course.

But it also means that, deep down, underneath how society interprets things, there *are* some definite answers. There are some things we definitely ought to do and some things we definitely ought not to do. These are the basic human Principles about things like helping other people, when to lie and how to punish people. In these areas, the prescriptions of right and wrong are still pure; they remain uninfected by the uncertainty of the situation. They tell us what we should do and we should do it.

This is much more than an academic curiosity. Widespread failure to understand right and wrong means death for people like Kintu. The misery in his village is preventable, and people need to understand that if 'should' means anything at all then we *should* stop his suffering. Whenever the words get confusing or the logic obscure, we should remember Kintu because helping him is what it's really all about. The origins of right and wrong may seem odd or alien; the endpoint is tragically human.

40 What to Do and Why

So this is what you should do:

1. Seek value.
2. Empathize, and be true to your obligations.
3. Help someone if your help is worth more to them than it is to you.
4. Treat people according to their own wants and intentions, not by what others want of them.
5. Let people choose for themselves, unless you know their interests better than they can.
6. Apply the Help Principle to others as much as they would apply it themselves.
7. Defend someone who was attacked without due reason as if you were attacked yourself.
8. Try to enjoy providing and receiving help in line with the Help Principle.
9. Help others with humility, and express gratitude for help you receive.
10. Ensure people who deliberately make bad things happen are punished as they should have been deterred, unless mercy is due.
11. Keep your promises unless changing to a new option is worth more than the trust and plans you waste.
12. Communicate so people can do what's best for the real circumstances.

13. In small groups, choose whichever option benefits any individual the most.

14. In large groups, choose whichever option has the best all-time outcome, by adding up the benefits and losses to people of each option.

15. Give three-quarters of 1 per cent of your income to tackle lethal poverty.

16. Contribute your fair share to solve common problems and encourage others to contribute their fair share too.

17. Help people more if you konw them or you owe them.

18. Respect good conventions and challenge bad ones.

19. Check your actions against your instincts; check your instincts are right for your situation.

20. Only do bad things to stop other people doing worse.

And here's why:

You should seek value in case it is there to be found. Indeed, seeking value *is* the meaning of life. And trying to find something really worth having or doing will involve using words like 'should' and 'ought'. If you don't believe 'should' and 'ought' relate to anything then you are in danger of leading a life lacking in value, a life without meaning, an empty life.

Using 'should' and 'ought' you will always be vulnerable to the 8-year-old who incessantly asks 'why?' For most reasons you give, she will be able to expose your response as circular, or that it just expresses authority, or ask 'why?' again. The only proper answer is to trace all your 'shoulds' and 'oughts' back to an unarguable source, and there are only two sources which can qualify – the twin virtues of empathy and obligation. These are the only virtues which match all we know about right and wrong. Any other basis for right and wrong is empathy or obligation by another name, or is no better than its equal and opposite, and the 8-year-old will be able to show your answer is empty. This is why empathy and obligation make up the double helix DNA of right and wrong.

Empathy and obligation also emerge if we take a more practical route from 'seek value'. We can show individuals need to follow rules to gain value from social interaction and the best way to follow the rules is to really believe in them, which means taking our obligations seriously. Being sociable is about *mutual* self-interest; it is about taking a real interest in others. People really do enjoy being nice to others. Empathy for others really is the route to value in life.

Empathy and obligation should direct all our interactions with others, including whether we interact at all. But this advice is too vague when we face complicated choices. We need a system for making decisions and that means clear guidelines on what we should try to make happen and the sorts of things we should do. This is where the Help Principle comes in since it guides both the actions we should perform and the consequences we should seek. The Help Principle descends from empathy and obligation in at least two ways, and it is the principle from which all others flow: we should help people when our help is worth more to them than it is to us – this is the basis for the first 14 principles set out above. Finally, when we reach the cloudy fringe of our predictive powers, where problems of information, certainty, complexity and the others mean we cannot project the principles onto the world without them becoming distorted, we must turn to conventions suited to our own time and space. Conventions adapt the principles to our own local worlds, and they account for the last of the 20 guidelines set out above.

So, there is no excuse – you ought to do what is right! You will improve lives, eradicate many bad things, and make the world a much, much better place.

This is right and wrong explained.

Selected Further Reading

Some ideas are too precious to be entrusted to a noble elite or encrypted for safe-keeping. Like sunlight and music, they should flow around the world, leaving silence and darkness only for people who choose them. Everybody should be allowed to play with ideas, to tumble them about, discuss them and distil them, until they have fixed upon the best.

Yet too many brilliant ideas are locked away, held captive by the way in which they are expressed. It used to be the Church which neutered thought by banning brilliant scientists like Galileo from publishing their discoveries. Nowadays, it is the coded communications of academics which wraps them in chains. Good thoughts are left to drown in their own jargon, ignored by the media and unknown to the public. The best way to rescue these vital thoughts is to explain them in lucid language, set out clearly and with examples people can easily understand. In the hope of resuscitating some great thoughts for a new audience, this list of selected further reading deliberately concentrates on more accessible material.

Part I – The Problem: We Need to Make Decisions, but We Don't Know How

Luke Rhinehart's *The Dice Man* is the disturbing yet entertaining portrayal of an overtly amoral life, and a warning of what we face if we abandon right and wrong completely. Thomas Paine's excellent *The Age of Reason* suggested that Christian ethics were just as arbitrary, a view echoed by atheist philosopher Bertrand Russell in his classic *Why I am not a Christian*, and Richard Dawkins in his modern best-seller *The God Delusion*.

Many of the early Enlightenment efforts to develop a new scientific approach to decision-making are harder to read. Bentham's *Principles of Morals and Legislation* is worthy but difficult; John Stuart Mill's *Utilitarianism* is better but still dense in places. For a good discussion of the pros and cons of the 'do whatever has the best consequences' decision-making system, try JCC Smart and Bernard Williams' *Utilitarianism: For and Against*. TH Green's *Prolegomena to Ethics* and Henry Sidgwick's *Method of Ethics*, both written in the language of their time, tried to domesticate this decision-making system with rules. For Kant, the best way to approach this Prussian genius is to read one of the many summaries of his work, such as Chapter 8 of Derek Johnston's *A Brief History of Philosophy* or Chapter 6 of Will Durant's wonderful *Story of Philosophy*; Kant's own *Fundamental Principles of the Metaphysic of Morals* and *Critique of Pure Reason* are only for the brave!

Part II – The Proof: Finding the Basis of Right and Wrong

The main points in this part will be covered in any good summary of 'meta-ethics' (the concepts behind and beyond ethics); Simon Blackburn's *Being Good* is a brilliant starting point for anyone interested in these issues, and Blackburn sets out his ideas more thoroughly in *Ruling Passions*. *Beyond Bumper Sticker Ethics* by Steve Wilkens offers an engaging account of why meta-ethics matters, while RM Hare's *Moral Thinking* offers a hefty defence of how codes of behaviour can improve quality of life. AC Grayling's *What is Good?* is more accessible, and

Stephen Law's *The Philosophy Gym* puzzles whether 'morality is like a pair of spectacles' in just ten ideas-packed pages.

Alastair MacIntyre's *After Virtue* locates right and wrong in characteristics, while GE Moore's defining work, *Principia Ethica*, attributes them to intuition, and Chapter 6 of AJ Ayer's *Language, Truth and Logic* downgrades them to mere exhortations of 'hurrah!' and 'boo!' *Ethics: Inventing Right and Wrong* by JL Mackie stands out as a book which both explains existing ideas and then takes them forward: he concludes, worryingly, that most ethical theories are based on an error. David Hume's ideas on ethics, which underpin so much in this field, are set out in his *An Enquiry Concerning the Principles of Morals* – if the old-fashioned language of this classic puts you off then start by reading an entry on the great man in any modern encyclopedia.

Part III – The Principle: Refining the Help Principle

John Rawls' *A Theory of Justice* reinvigorated moral and political philosophy in the 1970s. It is as important for the methods he outlines, such as his process of reflective equilibrium, as the conclusions he draws; he modified both in his later work, *Political Liberalism*. Rawls can be quite a heavy read, but there are several useful summaries of his work, such as within *John Rawls: His Life and Theory of Justice* by Thomas Pogge and Michelle Kosch.

Philip Turetsky's *Time* is a comprehensive investigation into just that. For a defence of letting people choose for themselves and a further example of trying to humanize 'do whatever has the best consequences' with good rules, there is probably still no better text than John Stuart Mill's *On Liberty*, although *An Intelligent Person's Guide to Liberalism* by Conrad Russell comes close. Reciprocity is covered very extensively in the highly entertaining *Prisoner's Dilemma* by William Poundstone. For a short but compelling argument which locates right and wrong in the intentions behind actions, read PF Strawson's article *Freedom and Resentment*. Peter Singer's *How Are We to Live?* is even more compelling, and explores our alarmingly broad responsibilities once we abandon the fiction that our actions are more important than our deliberate non-actions; Chapter 8 of that book also summarizes Maimonides' theory of charity rather neatly.

Part IV – The Programme: Extending the Principles to Other Problems

The problem of whether we have any wilful control of our actions is very old, but the explanations keep coming: Chapter 3 of Simon Blackburn's *Think* is one of the best new arrivals, covering the main points without overwhelming the reader. For more on the justifications for punishment you're best looking these up in an encyclopedia, such as the excellent Stanford Encyclopedia of Philosophy, which is online. Lies and promises form the basis of several paradoxes and these are often quite engaging – read *Paradoxes from A–Z* by Michael Clark to exercise your brain, or Roy Sorensen's *A Brief History of the Paradox* for a more thorough account. Martha Nussbaum's *Love's Knowledge* is probably the best bridge there is between analytic philosophy and the romantic themes of so much literature, and offers a far richer assessment of the philosophy of love than the cramped account in Chapter 27 of this book.

How groups should make decisions is the realm of political philosophy and Will Kymlicka's *Contemporary Political Philosophy* is an excellent summary of some of the main approaches in this field. For a chilling account of the dangers of making the individual entirely subservient to the group read George Orwell's unparalleled classic *Nineteen Eighty-Four*; to understand the absurd waste of groups directed entirely by individual self-interest, read *On Ethics and Economics* by Amartya Sen.

Part V – Practical Advice: For Real People in the Modern World

Thomas More's *Utopia* is more readable than most 500-year-old books, and the themes he raised have been taken up in lots of places since: try AC Grayling's *Life, Sex and Ideas* for a thoughtful discussion; *How to be Good* by Nick Hornby for an amusing novel on one person's attempt to turn Utopia into reality; and John Lennon's *Imagine* for inspiration.

Robert George's *The Autonomy of Law* dissects the complex relationship between legal and moral justice. Bernard Williams' theories are set out in his many lucid books: *Morality: An Introduction to Ethics* is true to its title; *Ethics and the Limits of Philosophy* is his classic work and includes his ideas on integrity; and his more recent *Moral Luck* is simply excellent. To appreciate Stoicism, including the advantages of defining responsibility narrowly and the pervasive impact of this ancient viewpoint on modern thought, read Tad Brennan's rounded and grounded *The Stoic Life*.

On development aid, Paul Collier's *The Bottom Billion* is radical and hard-edged, and Jeffrey Sach's book *The End of Poverty* offers the exciting prospect of ending poverty within our lifetimes. It is worth reading these alongside William Easterly's more cynical *White Man's Burden* for balance. Once you're satisfied that more can be done and that you should do a portion of it, *Our Day to End Poverty* by Shannon Daley-Harris, Jeffrey Keenan and Karen Speerstra offers some practical suggestions.

Part VI – The Prognosis: How to Make Good Decisions and Be Right All the Time

Our understanding of the world around us is probably much more limited than you might expect – www.philosophersnet.com offers a wide range of lucid and very readable articles about the limits of our knowledge including some quizzes and games, and is updated regularly. Read

Chapter 3 of Edward Lorenz's superb *The Essence of Chaos* to gauge the impossibilities of weather forecasting and Chapter 1 of Malcolm Gladwell's *The Tipping Point* for difficulties in predicting social trends. For a more optimistic assessment of our capacity to cope with problems of scale, uncertainty and complexity, explore James Surowiecki's *The Wisdom of Crowds*, which concludes with the enticing possibility of perfect foresight.

But that still leaves quantum effects, which seem as devastating as they are baffling. *Quantum: A Guide for the Perplexed* by Jim Al-Khalili is as clear an account as may be possible, and Stephen Hawking's *Brief History of Time* is the established market leader in explaining this dauntingly unexplainable subject. Einstein once tried to countenance some of the most bizarre implications of quantum physics by protesting 'God does not play dice!' – but if he was wrong, as this crazy branch of science seems to suggest, it may mean Luke Rhinehart had the best idea about right and wrong all along.

Index